I0801714

HONORING WORLD WAR CASUALTIES OF *Madison County, New York*

HONORING WORLD WAR CASUALTIES OF *Madison County, New York*

MATTHEW URTZ

THE History PRESS

Published by The History Press
Charleston, SC
www.historypress.com

First published 2022

Manufactured in the United States

ISBN 9781467143912

Library of Congress Control Number: 2022936215

This book is dedicated to my grandfathers, Gerald F. Botsford and Robert A. Urtz Sr., both World War II veterans.

CONTENTS

ACKNOWLEDGEMENTS

This book would not have been possible without the help of public libraries. It was originally started in 2017; however, a good portion was written throughout the COVID-19 pandemic. I wrote to public libraries throughout the Northeast to find newspaper accounts and specifically obituaries of soldiers who died while in service. Even in this age of digitization, local public libraries are still a very important source of knowledge and local history.

Our local public libraries have been excellent in providing information, and I would like to give a special thanks to all the library staff who assisted me along the way. Specifically, I'd like to thank Liz Metzger and Beth Totten of the Canastota Public Library, Betsy Kennedy and Elisha Davies of the Cazenovia Public Library, Joan Prindle of the Hamilton Public Library, Michelle Rounds of the Morrisville Public Library and Tom Murray of the Oneida Public Library. You all stepped up greatly to assist me, and I can never thank you enough.

Colgate University's special collections at Case Library held a world of information on students who served in both wars, as well as microfilm of the local newspapers. Sarah Keen and her staff were amazing to work with and always happy to help.

Our local historical societies and museums hold an abundance of information and provided me with a wealth of knowledge. Thank you to Sydney Loftus and Polly Held of the Madison County Historical Society; Christine O'Neil, Abigail Lawton and Tom Guiler of the Oneida Community Mansion House; Joe Digiorgio of the Canastota Canal Town

Museum; Elizabeth "Perk" Stalter of the Town of Brookfield Historical Society; Diane Van Slyke of the Town of Madison Historical Society; Celeste Smith of the Fryer Memorial Museum; and Laine Gilmore of the Erieville/Nelson Heritage Society. Madison County is lucky to have these institutions as well as others throughout our county providing historical resources and preserving the tales of those who came before us.

New York is unique in having local municipalities that appoint local historians, and Madison County has some amazing ones who assisted along the way. Some of these folks assisted me through their work with public libraries and historical institutions. Special thanks to the following historians: Elizabeth Stalter, Town of Brookfield; Sue Greenhagen, Village of Morrisville; Dick Sullivan and Charlie Albee, Village of Chittenango; Diane Van Slyke, Town of Madison; Fay Lyon and Laine Gilmore, Town of Nelson; Connie Coulthart, City of Oneida; Donna Burdick, Town of Smithfield; Mike Beardsley, Town of Sullivan.

To the historians across the state who took me under their wing when I started—people like Amie Alden of Livingston County, Gerry Smith of Broome County, John L. Scherer of the town of Clifton Park, Christine Ridarsky of Rochester and Peter Evans of Wayne County—thank you providing me with guidance and insight.

In Madison County, New York, I am lucky to be surrounded by great resources. The Madison County Veterans Agency was a wonderful source of assistance, and a special thanks goes out to its excellent staff, who have maintained their excellent service to the veteran community and were very responsive to my many questions. Thank you to former director Don Smith and current director Ronald Raymer, as well as Ellen Andros, Lukas Duimstra and Tamara Leggett.

This book would not have been possible without the support of the Madison County Attorney's Office, as well as the Madison County Board of Supervisors. County Administrator Mark Scimone and Public Information Officer Samantha Field both offered support and patience but would ask about the project on a regular basis, constantly showing their support. Thank you to Samantha and Emily Burns for your help in editing this project. I also want to thank former county administrator Paul Miller and former county clerks Ken Kunkel and Denise Roe for taking a chance on me and letting me grow into the role of historian. To current county clerk Michael Keville, who listened to my ideas and allowed me to run with them while providing thought provoking ideas and criticisms that have helped to make me better as a historian, thank you.

Thank you to Banks Smither, my acquisitions editor, for his never-ending patience and support for me writing this book during a pandemic.

Special thanks go to the people who read drafts of the book and offered insight into what could make it better. I was lucky to have such a wonderful group of authors and veterans to help make this project better. Thank you to Bruce Burke; Jim Coulthart; Norman Dann, PhD; Mike Kaiser; John Rathbone; and Milton Sernett, PhD.

To my parents, thank you for understanding my love of history and being okay with it. Thank you for allowing me to work part time at the family business until I could find a full-time position, and thank you for being you. To my siblings, thank you for asking for updates and being interested, even when I think you really were not.

To my wife, Christa, thank you for being willing to stop on a vacation to go to a museum or archive for "a few minutes," which were never that short. Thank you for your patience when I worked late into the night, when I was struggling to explain why I was frustrated and for your never-ending patience and support. I would have never completed this project without you.

INTRODUCTION

In 2016, I was trying to come up with a way to honor the upcoming World War I centennial. Madison County has a few great primary resources in our County Clerks Journal, which documented every soldier and nurse who left from Wampsville. Following the war in 1919, the *Oneida Dispatch* published a book, *Madison County's Welcome Home: In Honor of Her Sons and Daughters Who Served in the World War*. Both the Journal and *Madison County's Welcome Home* offered lists of soldiers, those who passed in service and a few personal accounts. This was my starting-off point; I was intrigued by the photos included of those who died while in service and decided that I would try to write a paragraph or two about each of those soldiers. As I dug deeper, I found that there were a lot of soldiers with significant ties to the county who were not included mostly because of where they lived. I decided that for this project to work, I wanted to include everyone who was:

- born in Madison County
- died in Madison County
- educated in Madison County (both grade school and college)
- worked in Madison County
- worshipped in Madison County
- buried in Madison County

I started to go down the rabbit hole, reading through microfilm newspapers to see what I could find out. During World War I, Madison County had at least eleven newspapers being published, many of these with complete sections dedicated to soldiers in service. While some soldiers were regularly referenced, others rarely showed up in local newspapers. In some cases, newspapers would publish letters from those in service, giving insight to what daily life was like. Occasionally, a letter would be published following the death of a soldier from an officer or a fellow soldier that would offer insight into what happened. For those who did not have a lot written about them, I would search through census records and military records available online to be able to have something on them. My goal was to give a little bit of information about their time before the war, their wartime experience and what happened after their death.

During this process, I attended a conference and spoke to some publishers about it, mostly for insight into how I could make it better. I was surprised to learn that there was some interest in publishing, but they all suggested that I include World War II as well.

As I started to write the World War II section, I had two realizations: first, there were too many stories for one book, and second, I knew the ending for almost every soldier. Whittling down the stories was hard but necessary; maybe someday I will write a second volume, or maybe I will look at stories of those who came home but were just as compelling—only time will tell. For this book, knowing that almost every story would end in the soldier's death could be heavy, especially when you read stories about soldiers never meeting their newborn children or stories where they died shortly before they were scheduled to go home. At times, I had to walk away and reset, but as I continued to research, I found captivating stories of bravery, exceptional stories of companionship and constant reminders of the sacrifice that these men and women made to make sure that we have the freedoms that we have today. I wanted to make sure that we had a record of these soldiers' stories so they are not forgotten. I hope the readers remember these individuals and the ultimate sacrifice that they made.

PART I
WORLD WAR I

On June 28, 1914, Archduke Franz Ferdinand, heir to the Austro-Hungarian throne, and his wife, Sofie, were assassinated in Sarajevo. One month later, on July 28, Austria-Hungary declared war on Serbia. Over the course of the next week, Russia, France, Belgium and Great Britain would side with Serbia to form the Allied Powers. Later, Italy, Japan and Portugal would join this alliance. The German Empire, Bulgaria and the Ottoman Empire would eventually joint together to form the Central Powers, and the sides were set.

President Woodrow Wilson stated that the United States would remain neutral, but a series of events would move the nation toward war. On May 7, 1915, the British ocean liner *Lusitania* was sunk by a German U-boat. A total of 1,198 passengers were killed in the attack, and that included more than 120 U.S. citizens, which caused significant outrage in the United States. Following the attack, President Wilson sent a letter demanding an end to attacking unarmed merchant ships, which Germany did until February 1, 1917.

On March 1, 1917, the "Zimmermann Telegram" was published across newspapers in America. The telegram, which was intercepted in January 1917 by British intelligence, was sent by German foreign secretary Arthur Zimmermann to Mexico, proposing an alliance if the United States declared war on Germany. President Wilson had learned of the existence of the telegram just a few days prior to the newspapers publishing it on February 26. The next day, Wilson proposed that the United States start arming its ships against possible German attacks. He also authorized the U.S. State Department to make the

Zimmermann Telegram public. On April 2, 1917, President Wilson went before Congress and presented his reasoning for declaring war on Germany; four days later, on April 6, 1917, the United States declared war on Germany.

In Madison County, New York, more than two thousand men and women served in the military or in the nursing corps during World War I. At the time of the 1920 census, Madison County had approximately forty thousand residents, meaning roughly 5 percent of Madison County's population served in some capacity in World War I. We know this from compiled lists of soldiers from New York State, local publications and the local county clerk register.

The Madison County Draft Board was formed on May 16, 1917.[1] The chairman of the board was Madison County sheriff Clarence G. Taylor. Madison County clerk Leonard L. Saunders served as the secretary, and Dr. George F. Mills was the surgeon. Dr. Mills resigned to accept a commission in the Army Medical Corps in August 1917.[2] Following Mills's resignation, Dr. Nelson O. Brooks replaced him in March 1918. Following Brooks's appointment, Sheriff Taylor stepped down, Saunders replaced him as chairman and B. Fitch Tompkins was appointed secretary. A number of additional positions on the board included chief clerk (Mrs. Addie B. Rockwell, Ms. Eva Ruth and Mrs. Matilda C. Saunders) and county appeal agent (the Honorable E.A. Kiley). Within this board there were two specialized boards that provided insight. The Legal Advisory Board was made up of the Honorable J.D. Senn, the Honorable E.A. Kiley and A.F. Devitt. The Medical Examining Board was made up of Dr. G.W. Davis, Dr. Donald Parker, Dr. Frederick Rommel, Dr. Frank C. Drake and Dr. A.V. Needham. The board registered 7,817 men, of which 1,103 were called to service. The board relied on the assistance of more than 700 volunteers during its service, which ended on March 31, 1919.

The Madison County Food Administration was started in January 1918 when W.D. Bartlett was sworn in as food commissioner.[3] Bartlett was responsible for keeping all food merchants in the county informed about food laws and making sure that those food laws were enforced. Bartlett also ordered sugar and issued weekly "fair price schedules." The administration worked with the Oneida Retail Grocer's Association and the N.Y.S. Troopers. During the year that the program existed, more than one hundred investigations were started based on complaints, and four criminal convictions for food violations were administered.

During the war, Madison County had five liberty bond issues, which raised almost $6.9 million, as well as raised more than $400,000 in War Savings Stamps.[4] In today's dollars, that would be approximately $125 million! Oneida postmaster Louis G. Quackenbush was the local director of war loans. The office was located at the Oneida Chamber of Commerce. Each of the five drives featured local chairpersons who covered the local towns, villages and hamlets. Quackenbush stated that he believed that "there are at least 18,000 persons in the county who own at least one Liberty Bond." That would mean almost half of the population of Madison County owned at least one bond.

At the start of World War I, the Red Cross was a fledgling organization.[5] The Oneida Chapter of the Red Cross was the first chapter organized in Madison County in April 1917. It was not long before branches opened in Oneida Castle, Stockbridge, Munnsville, Madison, Solsville, Bouckville, Durhamville, Higginsville, Sylvan Beach and West Vienna. Another chapter formed in southern Madison County and had branch offices in Hamilton, Morrisville and Cazenovia. The villages of Canastota and Chittenango aligned with the Syracuse chapter. The Red Cross not only helped the war effort, but it was also invaluable in assisting locally during the Spanish flu epidemic of 1918. The Oneida chapter sent nearly ninety-five thousand articles to Division Headquarters, while the Canastota branch produced close to seventy thousand articles for soldiers. The Oneida branch shipped more than eleven thousand pounds of used clothing to refugees.

Colleges in Madison County during the First World War adapted to the changes differently. Colgate University president Elmer B. Bryan placed the university at the disposal of the federal government.[6] The university brought in Canadian military officer Lieutenant Colonel Ballentine to take charge of the on-campus military training. Starting

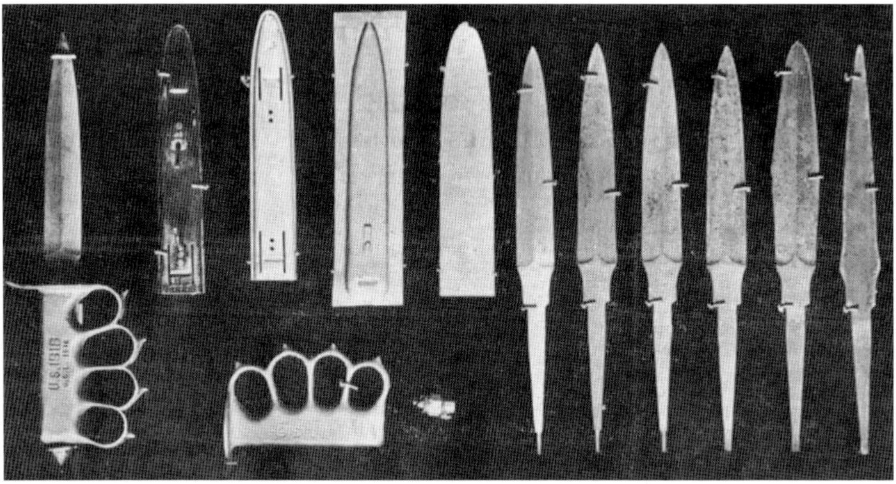

Various stages of construction of the trench knife, by Oneida Community Limited. Image taken from the Kenwood Chronicle. *Courtesy of the Oneida Community Mansion House.*

in September 1918, the government took over the college, dormitories were turned into barracks and nearly 400 students were mustered into the Student's Army Training Corps. Students were placed under the command of Major L.B. Lawton, who served in the Spanish-American War. The government operated the university until December 1918. At the outbreak of the war, Colgate had nearly 3,200 students and alumni in the United States, and more than one-fourth of those alumni served in the military during the war.

At the State School of Agricultural in Morrisville, a decrease in enrollment due to labor shortages led the college to change to a three-year program so that students would have more time to work on the farm.[7] School would start in October and end in April. Professors would visit students working on the farm during the summer and would speak with the employer on how the student was doing. The student would turn in a report in October describing the work they did while working on the farm.

During World War I, Oneida Community Limited converted to wartime production, completing war contracts close to $1.75 million (approximately $35 million in 2020 dollars).[8] The company made silverware, trench knives, periscopes, bolo handles, surgical tubes, magazine tubes and plated shells for the war effort. During the war, 276 Oneida Community men entered military service. Other employees served in the Red Cross or the YMCA. The board of directors voted that all married men and single men with dependents would receive full wages while they were in military service. Single men without dependents received half wages. During the war, 10 employees died while they were in service.

What follows next are brief accounts of the soldiers who lost their lives in their time of service during the great wars. We were not able to include everyone in this book, and maybe down the road we will do another including all those who were not. For now, I am including more than 50 World War I soldiers and more than 130 World War II soldiers.

The images that appear in this section are courtesy of the *Oneida Dispatch Press* unless otherwise noted.

BROOKFIELD

Jesse Lee Burdick

Birth: March 16, 1890, Columbus, New York[9]
Death: September 27, 1918, France
Burial: Brookfield Rural Cemetery, New York

Jesse Lee Burdick married Bessie A. Jaquay on June 30, 1911, in Brookfield.[10] They had two children, Donald and Nellie. Prior to being drafted, he was working as a farm laborer. He was inducted as a private on February 22, 1918, into Company I of the 305th Infantry. He went overseas in April 1918. He was seriously injured on August 22, 1918. While recovering, he was assigned to assist a squad that was behind the lines. He was killed in action when a shell burst over the squad he was assisting. The shell killed all but four men in the squad.

Howard Curtis

Birth: Around 1897, St. John's, Michigan[11]
Death: July 23, 1918, France
Burial: Columbus Corners Cemetery, New York

Prior to the war, Howard Curtis was living in South Edmeston and working as a farm laborer. His family moved to North Brookfield shortly thereafter.[12] He enlisted in the 17th Cavalry in Ohio in July 1915. He was transferred to Douglas, Arizona, for additional training at Fort Bliss and Chickamauga Park in Georgia before heading overseas in April 1918. Upon his arrival in France, he was transferred to the infantry. Curtis died four days after suffering wounds received in France during an Allied offensive.

Meade K. Palmer

Birth: May 20, 1897, Brookfield, New York[13]
Death: February 4, 1918, Portsmouth, Virginia
Burial: Brookfield Rural Cemetery, New York

Meade Palmer was a member of the First Baptist Church, superintendent of the Sunday school and church trustee, among other positions.[14] He enlisted in the U.S. Navy in October 1917. He trained as a gunner and then volunteered to become a firefighter, serving in Norfolk, Virginia, earning the rank of fireman, third class. Following his training, he was assigned to the USS *Illinois* in January 1918. He contracted cerebral-spinal fever on the ship and was transferred to the USS *Solace* Hospital Ship on February 2, 1918, and died two days later.

Carl C. Saunders

Birth: March 18, 1896, Brookfield, New York[15]
Death: February 24, 1919, France
Burial: Leonardsville Cemetery, New York

Carl Saunders graduated from local schools in 1915 and entered Colgate University, majoring in chemistry.[16] Saunders was inducted as a private into Company C of the 310th Infantry on September 8, 1917.[17] He was assigned to Camp Dix. Saunders was transferred to the Headquarters Company of the 310th Infantry. He was promoted to third class musician in May 1918 and band corporal in November of the same year. He was sent overseas in May 1918. He wrote about the trip in June:

> *We have arrived safely and are now quartered in what was formerly a fine summer resort. The buildings were big apartment houses I should judge and perhaps the summer places of the quite well-to-do. The buildings are all of stone and seven or eight stories in height. I am up in the sixth story and sleeping on the bare floor, but it goes much better than it did on shipboard where it was so stuffy one could hardly get a fresh breath at all.*
>
> *We had quite a little excitement last Sunday. We were attacked by submarines while we were eating supper about 5 pm. The attack lasted three hours, during which time we saw quite some excitement. We are sure of having sunk two submarines and think we sank the third while our ships escaped without injury. One submarine stuck its periscope up not over a hundred yards from our ship and almost under the bow of the boat ahead of us. It was immediately pounced upon by a destroyer and put out of business by a depth bomb.*
>
> *Another one was sunk some hundred yards back of us, while still a third was sunk but a short distance on our right. As five submarines were reported to have been seen at about 3 o'clock in the afternoon, they are probably the ones that attacked us. Aside from that little incident the trip was void of excitement.*[18]

Saunders took part in the campaigns at Saint-Mihiel and Meuse-Argonne, as well as the Battle of Vimy. He wrote about training experiences:

> *Today we had a 10-mile hike. During our hike we stopped at a gas school and were issued gas masks and had a 5 minute test in a gas chamber to see if our gas masks were all ok. I should hate to have to wear one very long. My head seemed bursting before we were allowed to remove them. Perhaps and very probably because they fit so tightly. Anyway I hope we won't be compelled to wear them much.*

In a later letter, he stated:

> *I can hear an aeroplane humming over my head as I write. We see any number of them every day. They are constantly going back and forth overhead. I think I would like to take a little ride in one myself. I should think it would be good sport after one got used to being up so high.*

In his last letter home from January 1919, he spoke about getting leave and spending time in Monte Carlo and other French cities while on leave:

> *You'll undoubtedly be surprised when you read the heading of my letter but it's the truth. I'm in Monte Carlo and have been for almost a week.*
>
> *The men in our company were told to put in their names for a seven days leave, exclusive of travel. As I was eligible, I put mine in and won out. Our train left Semur, where I'm stationed, at four o'clock Sunday night and we got here about Tuesday morning about nine o'clock. You can readily see it was quite a ride, though, of course, we traveled rather slowly (speed isn't the middle name of most of the French trains). We passed through Dyon, Lyons and Marseilles, Nice and several other big towns on the way. Between Lyons and Marseilles the scenery, in some places, is almost like the Palisades.*
>
> *On arriving at Monte Carlo, I was assigned to Le Grand Hotel, the second best in the city. After being up North in the mud and sleeping on stone floors, I can't kick even a little bit. The room, which I share with another fellow, is fine. We have a private bath, in fact everything necessary for physical comfort. It is certainly tough to lie abed till eight thirty or nine o'clock, then get up and go down to breakfast without a mess kit under one's arm.*[19]

Saunders ultimately contracted a fatal case of meningitis.

CHARLES B. VUNK

Birth: March 8, 1900, Columbus, New York[20]
Death: February 18, 1919, Rhode Island
Burial: Unadilla Forks Cemetery, New York

Charles Vunk's family moved to Brookfield, where he attended local schools. Following graduation, he entered the Morrisville School of Agriculture, which he attended until the war started. He returned home to work on his family's farm, as he did not reach the required enlistment age until after the war had ended. On February 3, 1919, as soon as he was eligible, Vunk entered the navy and was sent to a training station in Newport, Rhode Island. He died of pneumonia in Rhode Island.

CAZENOVIA

Hubert Butts

Birth: June 11, 1895, Plymouth, New York[21]
Death: October 24, 1918, Syracuse, New York
Burial: New Woodstock Cemetery, New York

Hubert Butts moved with his family to Cazenovia in 1907. He attended business school in Binghamton and was working in Syracuse when he was drafted in September 1918. He was assigned to Camp Syracuse and was appointed an inspector for the government. He worked at the Franklin Manufacturing Company, which was producing planes, in Syracuse for a roughly a week before he contracted influenza. He died from the influenza.

Arthur H. Reeves

Birth: January 16, 1889, Medina, New York[22]
Death: October 19, 1918, Virginia[23]
Burial: Palmyra Cemetery, New York

Prior to the war, Arthur H. Reeves attended Cazenovia Seminary. He married Miss Florence G. Turverey in Cazenovia on December 17, 1918.[24] He was living in East Harpswell, Maine, working as a farmer when he enlisted in the Commissioned Officer Training School.[25] He was assigned to Camp Lee in Petersburg, Virginia, where he died after contracting Spanish influenza.

EATON

Andrew Branagan

Birth: Around 1896, West Eaton, New York[26]
Death: October 10, 1918, Fort Jay, New York
Burial: West Eaton Cemetery, New York

Prior to the war, Andrew Branagan was working as a farm laborer.[27] He enlisted in Vermont as a private in Company B of the 22nd Infantry on April 13, 1917. He was transferred to the Headquarters Company of the 22nd Infantry in August 1918. Branagan was promoted to private first class in June 1918 and corporal in September 1918. Branagan died at Fort Jay (New York) of pneumonia.

Leland Mead

Birth: November 16, 1887, Morrisville, New York[28]
Death: October 4, 1918, France
Burial: Meuse-Argonne American Cemetery & Memorial, France; Memorial to Theodore & Leland, Morrisville Rural Cemetery, New York

After attending local schools, Leland Mead attended Mercersburgh Academy in Pennsylvania for a year but was forced to withdraw due to illness. He moved to Arizona to convalesce and then came back home for a period.

Around 1910, Leland moved to Kiesling, Washington, and maintained an apple orchard there. He enlisted in November 1917 and was transferred to the Medical Corps. He was transferred overseas in July 1918. He served on the front lines in the Medical Corps. On October 3, 1918, Leland was working in an aid station in the Argonne Forest. Despite being heavily shelled, the men working in the aid tent had just evacuated the last of the wounded when a shell struck the aid tent and nearly took off one of Mead's legs. Captain Paul F. Brown sent a letter to his family explaining what happened:

> *It is with sorrow that I have to tell you that Private Leland C. Mead of our detachment was severely wounded on Oct. 3rd and died the next day.*
>
> *Private Mead was one of our best men, an excellent soldier, and we feel his loss very much. He was especially loyal to me and a hard worker, and I feel a personal loss in his death. I wish to extend to you my deepest sympathy.*
>
> *On the afternoon of Oct. 3rd he was helping me in an aid station in the Argonne forest. We were under terrific shell fire and had many wounded to care for. About 5 pm when we had just evacuated our last wounded, Private Mead was standing beside me talking when a shell came through our aid station and nearly took off one of his legs.*
>
> *We took care of him immediately and carried him back to our rear aid station, from which he was evacuated to field hospital No. 12, First division. He died at 2:50 the next morning. Private Mead was buried at Cheppy Sur Meuse.*[29]

THEODORE F. MEAD

Birth: June 29, 1885, Morrisville, New York[30]
Death: October 29, 1918, France
Burial: Meuse-Argonne American Cemetery & Memorial, France; Memorial to Theodore & Leland, Morrisville Rural Cemetery, New York

Theodore Mead graduated from Morrisville schools and then attended Cornell University, graduating in 1908.[31] He returned to Cornell Medical School, graduating in 1913. He married Lena R. Fahnestock of Ithaca in 1912. They had a daughter, Elizabeth, born around 1916. He studied in New York City at Belleview Hospital under Dr. Goodrich and accepted a position there upon his graduation. In June 1916, he volunteered in the

First Field Artillery and was stationed at the United States–Mexican border, before he was mustered out in November 1916. He was commissioned a first lieutenant in the Medical Corps after completing officer's school in Plattsburg in June 1917. He was stationed at Camp Wadsworth (South Carolina) and at Camp Stuart (Virginia) before being sent overseas in June 1918. He was promoted to captain in March 1918. He was assigned to the 104th Field Artillery. Letters to his wife were published in November 1918 explaining some of his experiences:

> *Life has been so many things after another recently that letter-writing has been impossible. I am now seated at a rough wooden table on a little wooden stool in a spacious underground room with lots of music from the big guns. I have not seen anything or anybody but soldiers for more than three weeks and have no connection to the outside world…*
>
> *My first home at the front was a very satisfactory one, but not in the most ideal location. I cannot describe it to you for good reasons. Its location, however, was under a graveyard just outside a small shattered town. Recollect some of the pictures shown in the picture supplement of the Sunday Times and you can reconstruct the village. Not a building had escaped. The poor old graveyard had fared little better and I venture to say not a dozen stones have escaped injury, and many were in fragments, and a large cross had been broken at the base but still remained erect, being held by a heavy iron pin set in the base stone and extending up through a vertical shaft. This would rock back and forth in the wind at night with a most uncanny sound.*
>
> *The trench rats came up to all expectations, both as to the size, number and tameness. After a short while no one even chases the poor fellows and strike up a fair partnership with them.*[32]

Major George Augustine wrote to Mrs. Mead about Theodore's death in December 1918:

> *The Regiment had been in rest billets for a few days after having been constantly in the line since Sept. 9th, expecting to remain there for three weeks. But on Oct. 28th the regiment was again was ordered into action.*
>
> *The end battalion, your husband as battalion surgeon, left the rest camp on the morning of the 28th and advanced north of Verdun. That night it crossed to the east side of the Meuse, and early on the morning of the 29th took up a position east of the village of Brabant.*

Captain Mead established his aid post and went to battalion headquarters dugout. He left this station shortly after 11 am to return to his aid post. At just this time the enemy began to shell the road very heavily and before the captain and his orderly Marvin, who was with him, could seek shelter a shell fragment struck the captain in the upper right arm.

This was on October 29th at 11:30 am. Marvin immediately cut the clothes away from the wound and applied a shell dressing which stopped all hemorrhage. At 11:45 an ambulance and medical officer came. The officer examined the arm and administered an opiate in preparation for the long ride to the evacuation hospital at Verdun, twenty kilometers away. The captain was fully conscious at the time. The shell fragment had broken the arm, but we thought that was the most serious part of his wound. I did not see him myself, not coming up to the position with regimental headquarters until that afternoon.

We heard nothing more of the captain, the regiment remaining in action until the armistice was signed and not returning to Verdun until November 19th.

The next day I went to the evacuation hospital at Glorieux just outside of Verdun to see what base hospital Captain Mead had been evacuated, as I wanted to get in touch with him.

I was dismayed to learn that the ambulance had arrived at the hospital at 1:45 and that the officers then had found the captain in shock and that he died at 2:20 pm less than three hours after he was hit.

I could not believe it until I had examined the records and finally found his final resting place with his identification tag fastened to the cross at the head of the grave.

It was a terrible shock to me to learn that the captain was dead instead of on the road to recovery, as we had every reason to believe he would be. A piece of shell had evidently passed through the upper arm and into the chest. The officers at the hospital told me that he did not suffer but gradually and calmly went to sleep. He rests in the section of the large military cemetery at Glorieux, a short distance outside of Verdun.[33]

JASPER SMITH

Birth: February 1893, West Eaton, New York[34]
Death: October 13, 1918, France
Burial: West Eaton Cemetery, New York

Jasper Smith's grandmother Mrs. Phebe Smith adopted him as a child.[35] Prior to the war, Jasper was working as a farm laborer.[36] He was inducted as a private in Company L of the 305th Infantry on February 22, 1918.[37] He was sent overseas in April 1918. He was wounded by a piece of shrapnel overseas but recovered from those injuries and was released.[38] Not long after he was released, Smith contracted pneumonia and died.

Percy D. Westcott

Birth: September 6, 1895, Cazenovia, New York[39]
Death: September 25, 1918, France
Burial: Oise-Aisne American Cemetery and Memorial, France; Memorial at Morrisville Rural Cemetery, New York

Percy Westcott enlisted in Company G of the Marine Corps on May 24, 1917. He was sent overseas on July 3, 1917. Westcott wrote a series of letters after he went overseas. His first letter talks about what it was like during the trip overseas:

> *Perhaps some of you can imagine how I felt to be out of sight of land entirely, be aboard ship for the first time.*
>
> *The first fish I saw were dolphins (about three or four feet long). Later I saw a shark and several whales and they were some fish I can tell you; a bit larger than the suckers and other fish I caught in the Chenango at home. I also saw black fish (eight to twelve feet long), and when we crossed the Gulf Stream I saw some flying fish, which would sail on their wings a short distance and drop into the water again. We also saw some sailfish and other queer objects. There were two or three days in mid-ocean when we saw no gulls. We saw some ships but can't tell you much about them or some other things to present, although if God spares me to return to you all I will try and remember some of the things that will not pass censor at this time.*[40]

He also wrote about traveling:

> *Except for the risk of life there is no better job if a man likes to travel and see some of the world.*

In the following letter, he references the spring-like weather they were having that winter and the local men with whom he was serving.[41] He wrote to a friend on August 26, 1918:

> *I received your welcome letter with clippings enclosed a few days ago. I have also just received word from mother of the severe storm near home. Storms do a lot of damage but can't be compared to a hail of shot and shell. My brother used to speak of you when he worked near there so I am glad to hear from you. My experiences have been in many respects similar to those of Al Karpp who is also over here (that you mentioned). But I differ with him in that I believe the Red Cross is the lead with a helping hand, and I think Soldier Karpp will find it so after he has a turn in active warfare. The Red Cross certainly deserves all the praise the boys of the A.E.F. can give them. U.S. Boys all greatly appreciate that the Red Cross, "Y" and other such organizations are doing for their benefit. But greater than that do we value the ever-welcome letters, etc., from mother, relatives and friends, as they are always full of good cheer and anxious thoughts for our welfare as well as the cheering news of what the folks back home are doing to provide for us and back us up for the winning of the war in favor of democracy and humanity for the generations of future civilization and peace.*
>
> *I have seen men make the supreme sacrifice, one such being our friend Lloyd Evans of the marines. I was only slightly acquainted with him and saw him only a few days before he received his deathblow. He was in the regiment next to mine but I did not see very much of him. It seems hard to see a friend from near one's hometown pay the penalty, but his people have my deepest sympathy, as I know what he had to go through. His name may well be placed on the honor roll as one of the Hamilton boys who gave his life for his country. I guess there are many Madison County boys now in France, but I have not met any, as I know of yet…*
>
> *The winters only last about four to six weeks, but rain takes the place of snow except in December and January. I have experience both in open and trench warfare. Also had the rats, cooties, etc. to contend with, rats being the most plentiful in the trenches. Last winter I had the good luck to shoot a red fox but since then I have added to my list of legal game. Ha! Ha!*

> *I was very much pleased with the way Madison County went "over the top" with*

the Liberty Loan and Red Cross subscriptions, which same play so great a part in our success over here. I, too have five $50 Liberty bonds, all paid by allotment in July. I would take out more but I think I'll have the allotment made over to mother to invest in Thrift Stamps or use for her own comforts as she sees fit. I have $5,000 insurance with Uncle Sam just as a protection against the future. Uncle Sam takes good care of his boys. I'm sure proud that I am a Yankee, whether I'm a "Devil Dog" or a U.S. marine or any kind of soldier so long as I am doing my duty by home and country. As we will be drawing full pay next pay day I hope to create an interest among the boys to adopt one of those French orphans. I don't mean an Mlle. (by marriage), only a young child. Ha! Ha! I am proud that dear mother whose prayers have brought me safely through battles. I greatly appreciate the beautiful service flag she has for me. I mean to keep morally clean, honest and do my duty, and deserve her prayers that the honor may be hers. I believe it is harder for those that must stay at home than for those that have the opportunity to serve on the bloody battle fields of France.

Well, we are looking forward to the day when this strife shall be over. Hoping this has not tried the patience of the good censor. I'll close hoping to hear from you and others. Meanwhile I'll keep fighting until Niagara Falls and Kaiser Bill are busted. Ha! Ha! With good luck and best regards. Your sincere soldier friend.[42]

Westcott died of scarlet fever.

FENNER

Lloyd H. Stoker

Birth: March 9, 1889, Cazenovia, New York[43]
Death: October 6, 1918, France
Burial: Evergreen Cemetery, Cazenovia, New York

Lloyd Stoker grew up in Fenner and was working as a farm laborer in the area before moving to Akron, Ohio. While in Ohio, he worked for the Goodrich Company.[44] He was inducted as a private into Company I of the 1st Infantry Replacement Regiment on May 27, 1918, in Akron.[45] Stoker was assigned to Camp Gordon in Georgia. He was then transferred to Company E of the 59th Infantry in August 1918. He was sent overseas in July 1918. Stoker was killed by wounds he received in action.

HAMILTON

William A. Anderson

Birth: July 31, 1888, Boston, Massachusetts[46]
Death: July 18, 1918, Unknown
Burial: Unknown

William Alwin Anderson's parents died at a young age, and he does not appear to have had any siblings or close relatives. Prior to the war, he was working as an auditor for a telephone company in Weehawken, New Jersey. He enlisted at Colgate University as part of the class of 1917. At the outbreak of the war, he attempted to gain a commission, unsuccessfully. He went to Canada and obtained a commission as a lieutenant in the Aviation Squadron.[47] He trained as a member of the Royal Flying Squadron and left for England in March 1918. While in England, he visited the grave of a fellow Colgate alum. According to a letter, he had to fly over enemy lines. On July 18, 1918, Anderson flew into France at the start of an Allied offensive; his plane did not return.[48] It is unknown if his plane crashed or how he died; his burial location is also unknown.

Robert B. Baker

Birth: October 3, 1887, Hamilton, New York[49]
Death: October 8, 1918, Philadelphia, Pennsylvania
Burial: Earlville Cemetery, New York

Robert Blaine Baker graduated from Colgate University in 1912.[50] He married Miss Zella Lewis on March 16, 1918.[51] His brother Kenneth served in the navy during the war. Prior to the war, he was working as an inspector with the Brown-Lipe Gear Company. He was inducted as a private into the 348th Infantry on June 23, 1918. In August of that year, he was transferred to the Gas Defense Division of the Chemical Warfare Service. He was assigned to a gas plant in Philadelphia, where he worked as an inspector. Baker died of pneumonia in Philadelphia.

William B. Brown

Birth: January 17, 1890, Hamilton[52]
Death: November 5, 1918, France
Burial: France

William B. Brown grew up in Hamilton but moved to Pennsylvania around 1912. Prior to moving, Brown worked as a clerk at Root's drugstore. He was inducted as a private in Company B of the 305th Motor Supply on February 13, 1918. In April 1918, he was transferred to Company D. He was sent overseas in May 1918. Brown died from heart disease. His family received a letter that explained his death:

> *We left the "truck park" on November 3rd, am with rations for the boys at the front. About noon, your brother and I were taken sick from the gas fumes from the motor. We ate a cold lunch as we traveled but neither of us could eat much, we traveled till well into the night, when the roads got so rough that we couldn't go any longer as were not allowed to have any lights and it was cloudy and raining. We slept in the truck that night, without any supper, at daylight on the fourth we proceeded without a cup of coffee. We were supposed to have reached our destination before but the enemy was retreating so fast and our boys were advancing so that we could not overtake them. The roads were very bad too, for several hours we remained in one*

place with our truck stuck in a "shell hole." We were compelled to unload in order to get out. Our cargo consisted of three tons of bacon, so you can see this was no small proposition for us two. We had nothing to eat for most two days and were still sick from the cause mentioned before. We reached Buzancy at about 5 PM on the fourth when we were informed that we had several miles more to travel in order to get the rations to the boys at the front. At about 7 PM our gas tank ran dry. Your brother was on the seat by my side, the seat was not wide so he had laid down about one hour before this and went to sleep. I had noticed snoring time after time and thought how much good the few minutes sleep was doing him when my tank ran dry. As it was under the seat, I tried to waken your brother so we could fill the tank, and I shook him several times. No reply. I called some engineers that were working on the road nearby and we worked on him for some time but it did no good. You can imagine how I felt. My comrade dying there on the seat by my side and I not knowing it. I spent the night here with him, all alone. The next morning I went to the next town where they had a field hospital. Here they had taken your brother and buried him. The name of the town was Vaus, not far from the Meuse River about fifty miles northwest of Verdun.[53]

Raymond D. Cockett (also Crockett)

Birth: Around 1896, New York[54]
Death: April 21, 1918, Brooklyn, New York[55]
Burial: Hamilton Center Cemetery, Hamilton, New York

Raymond D. Cockett grew up in southern Madison County. Following the death of his father in August 1914, his family moved to Sauquoit in Oneida County.[56] He enlisted from Sauquoit into the navy in November 1917 and served as a yeoman and fireman second class.[57] He spent his entire service time in and around New York City. Raymond was diagnosed with diphtheria while serving at the Brooklyn Navy Yard. He was taken to a hospital but died of pneumonia.[58]

Vinton Adams Dearing

Birth: January 2, 1896, Yokohama, Japan[59]
Death: July 18, 1918, France
Burial: Oise-Aisne American Cemetery & Memorial, France

Vinton Dearing's father was a clergyman and worked at a seminary. They may have been missionaries in Japan. He graduated from Colgate University in 1917. While there, he was a member of Beta Theta Pi fraternity, the track team and a number of other clubs.[60] He enlisted in Massachusetts and trained at Madison Barracks in Sackets Harbor, New York. Dearing earned a commission as a lieutenant. He was awarded a Distinguished Service Cross by order of General Pershing for

> *detailed in command of a carrying party, May 28th, near Cantigny he bravely proceeded under fire to execute his mission and by his example of bravery heartened his men who were under fire at the time. On May 29th, Lieutenant Dearing took his party through heavy shell fire to carry ammunition to the front lines without being ordered to do so.*[61]

On July 14, 1918, he served as an aide to General Pershing in the Bastille Day Parade in Paris. Just four days later, Dearing was killed in action at the second battle of Marne in France.

A Colgate classmate, Lieutenant Morris Andrews, said of him:

> *In fighting of this kind a man is either all yellow dog or all man. Vinton Dearing was all man.*[62]

Lloyd V. Evans

Birth: September 24, 1898, Hamilton, New York[63]
Death: June 17, 1918, France
Burial: Woodlawn Cemetery, Hamilton, New York

Lloyd Evans and his brother, Harold, served in the military. Lloyd attended local schools and moved to Detroit, Michigan, where he was working at the motor works prior to enlisting. He enlisted in the Marine Corps in April 1917.

He was trained as a machine gunner. He traveled to France in October 1917. Evans wrote his mother on April 15, 1918:

> *It is a wonder that I am writing this now in such a place as this. We have damp dugouts to sleep in and when we are not standing a gun watch, almost everyone is sleeping. The trench mud is nearly a foot deep in some places. Another nice thing we have to contend with is gas—we have had five gas alarms in one night to break up what little sleep we do get—when it is given, it is on with your masks and outside your toes. The Germans bombard us nearly every day.*
>
> *Yesterday PM I had to make a trip of about two and a half miles to our headquarters. The route led me along a camouflaged path into a destroyed French Town. From there a communication trench leads up a hill and ends at the edge of a big wood. From there I followed a wood road, which took me into headquarters. Now to come back to the shelling I was almost into the town following this camouflaged path when the first shell hit one of the stone buildings. I dropped onto my stomach in the grass and waited while the Boches threw about twelve high explosive shells and two gas shells into the town. Things certainly were being torn up there for awhile. I could hear pieces of rock and shrapnel landing on the ground around not far from me. After it was over I went on through. I stayed up to headquarters last night and a little after two this morning they started another bombardment and kept it up until about nine. They brought one wounded French soldier in but I guess he was about all that got hurt.*
>
> *I started back for the position about ten and there were all kinds of shell holes along the path. In one place down a in a little hollow I ran into quite a bit of gas. From our positions, we can see quite a few destroyed French towns. Only a very few houses in any of these town have roofs on them.*
>
> *Just to think that about four years ago these were pretty little towns, the people living a nice quiet life in them, makes me hate the Kaiser all the more.*[64]

Evans wrote about daily life on May 7, 1918:

> *As it is, a detail of three men is picked three times a day to hike back through a muddy communication trench to headquarters, after bacon and spuds, (jackets on) for breakfast, maybe beef and gravy with spuds (jackets on) for dinner and slum-m-m-m, maybe for supper, or, at least once a day. It has been soup so far, for some time past, as the galley force hasn't been able to get any flour to thicken it with. This menu varies from time to time,*

> *but this is the general hand out. This naturally becomes monotonous and the sweet stuff is missed very much. In some rest camps we can get at Y.M.C.A.'s and buy things, but they are more scarce in these parts than the people back in the states think, and we are generally in the trenches more than we are at these places. The last place we were at, the nearest Y.M.C.A. I knew about was three miles away and we haven't had a pay day since March 12, only a few went over.*
>
> *For the first few days after we hit the rest camps, all we do is clean up, eat and sleep, but a few days before we leave, we catch working parties every night. We start about eight o'clock and hike back in towards the lines about three or four miles and dig trenches for hours and then start back. Oh, it is a great life, I'll say! And everyone of those slackers back there in the states, working at soft jobs, having a good time, making big money, ought to be over here too, it would do them damn good. A while ago, back at the rest camp, I ran into a fellow who told me that Harold's outfit was at a place about twenty miles away, and I have wondered if he could be over here.*[65]

On May 24, 1918, he made a note in a letter to his mother that there was a reason he had not written more recently and he would explain it later. Shortly after that letter, Lloyd died of wounds received in France.

HOWARD EDWARDS HAWKINSON

Birth: October 30, 1890, Minnesota[66]
Death: October 8, 1918, France
Burial: Meuse-Argonne American Cemetery & Memorial, France

Howard Hawkinson was a student at Colgate University, part of the 1912 class and a member of the Theta Psi fraternity. In the summer of 1916, Hawkinson took the Regular Army Officer exams in Plattsburg. He was commissioned a second lieutenant in Company I of the 28th Infantry in March 1917 and promoted to captain in April 1918. He trained at Camp Leavenworth (Kansas) and served at the Mexican border until the end of May, when he was sent overseas arriving in June 1917. He fought in the Meuse-Argonne Campaign, Montdidier-Noyon Campaign and the Battles of Aisne-Marne and Saint-Mihiel. He was injured when he was shot in the leg in July 1918 during the Battle of Soissons. He was killed in action while attempting to stop a German machine gun attack with an empty revolver on

October 8, 1918. He was posthumously awarded the Distinguished Service Cross and a Silver Star for gallantry in action. The medals were achieved for the capture and holding of the French town of Cantigny. Following Hawkinson's death, a large article was published about his time in the service compiled from his letters and the letters of his fellow soldiers that explained a number of these events. The Distinguished Service Cross was bestowed on him for his actions in capturing the French town of Cantigny on May 1918; he wrote prior to the battle:

> *Just now we are on the threshold of great things. I expect this will be my last chance to write for some time to come, I am part of that portion of the American Army, which has been given a post of very great honor. We are on our toes to show our mettle alongside our allies.*

Of the battle, he wrote:

> *I have seen something of war in the last ten months, but this that we face now is far beyond anything the people at home can ever imagine. By the time this reaches the states I may have received the "Croix d Guerre" or the "Croix de Bois" or both. In case it is the latter, you'll know I got up in the midst of the scrap. I am going strong these days.*

A soldier wrote about Hawkinson's injury briefly:

> *On swept the men of the 28th Infantry: over the hills right in among the abandoned guns of the German batteries. Captain Hawkinson suddenly came upon a 77 field piece, still hot and smoking with a pile of fused shells at his side. It appears to be intact and yielding to the temptation in the excitement of the fight he switched the piece around with the aid of a couple of his men, sending a dozen shells screaming after the retreating gunners.*
>
> *A little later Major Tack of the 3d battalion fell, and Captain Hawkinson succeeded to command, though he never received the title. Major Tack was badly wounded and Captain Hawkinson had received a machine gun bullet in the leg. He dressed the wound himself and refused to go to the rear.*

A soldier wrote about the day Hawkinson died after a night of serious fighting and casualties:

> *In the dim morning light they could vaguely distinguish in the fog, the outlines of a body of men—some thirty in number—standing boldly in the open a hundred yards or so away. Thinking they were men from one of his own companies who had lost their bearings Hawkinson led the way toward them. Not until within a few yards of them did he discover them to be enemy troops. They had been allowed to approach unchallenged as they themselves had been mistaken for a returning patrol. The surprise was mutual.*
>
> *It was not time for hesitation and hopelessly outnumbered there seemed to be nothing else to do but to attempt a ruse. Captain Hawkinson drew his automatic and rushed straight at the bewildered group, shouting and shooting in their midst while the other five quickly followed his lead. The Hun, taken off his guard and thinking that the Americans were attacking quickly surrendered.*
>
> *But, at the instance the hands went up, two of the prisoners suddenly detached themselves and ran back into the darkness. Captain Hawkinson guessed that they were trying to reach a machine gun in the woods. He gave chase toward the far side of the clearing in an effort to out flank them, and as his only weapon was an empty "45," he had little opportunity to make them halt.*
>
> *Lieutenant Garrit, the liaison officer, also realizing the danger, followed at a distance of fifty feet, leaving Birmingham and the runners to guard the prisoners. The Boche, however had too great a lead and were able to reach and put the gun into action before either of the Americans could prevent. Hawkinson slipped into a shell hole and fell, just in a position to receive, point blank, at twenty yards most of the contents of the gunner's magazine. Garrit was within a few yards of the men when they swung their weapon and got him too. The piece then jammed and the gunners made their escape.*

His brother Jack was also a commissioned officer; Jack was wounded while serving.[67]

Michael Joseph Hayes

Birth: September 5, 1894, Youngstown, Ohio[68]
Death: October 14, 1918, France
Burial: Arlington National Cemetery, Virginia

Michael J. Hayes was the 1918 class president while he was at Colgate University.[69] He played on multiple sports teams and clubs. He was commissioned a second lieutenant of Company F of the 306th Infantry on August 15, 1917. He was promoted to first lieutenant in January 1918. He trained at the Plattsburgh Barracks and Camp Upton in New York. Hayes went overseas in April 1918. He served in the Battles of Oisne-Aisne and Meuse-Argonne. Hayes received the Distinguished Service Cross; his citation reads:

> *For repeated acts of extraordinary heroism at Bazoches, August 13th, 1918 and St. Juvin, October 14th, 1918. On a patrol of five men in broad daylight and without any cover rescued his company commander who had fallen wounded near a German machine-gun nest. Failing to find the wounded officer, he crawled to within twenty yards of the post, attacked it with great dash and gallantry inflicting a number of casualties in spite of heavy fire from enemy machine guns and hand grenades. On October 14 this officer in the face of direct fire from the enemy upon his platoon, disregarding his own personal safety, went forward to reconnoiter and find cover for his men from which to continue the attack. In the performance of his courageous enterprise he was killed.*[70]

Arthur Seward Moran

Birth: August 20, 1893, Syracuse, New York[71]
Death: October 17, 1918, France
Burial: Forest Park Cemetery, Camden, New York

Arthur Moran was part of Colgate University's class of 1917 and a member of Phi Gamma Delta fraternity.[72] Prior to the war, he worked for the *Camden Advance-Journal*. He joined Troop M of the First New York Cavalry (National Guard) as a private on June 12, 1917.[73] He was promoted to private first class in October 1917 and was transferred to Company D of the 105th Machine Gun Battalion in March 1918, training in Spartanburg, South Carolina. Moran was sent overseas in May 1918. He wrote to his mother in October 1918:

> *The writing I get done now must be during the short intervals that we stop to eat. Believe me we are going some on the heels of old Fritz.*

I was in school when we pulled off our first real stunt but I came back just in time for this one is regular. We are having mostly open fighting now—its fun to see them fall. It would be better if they were the only ones that got it but that is part of the game.

"Moose" is in the hospital with a bit of shrapnel in the arm but he is not bad; lucky boy, gets a rest.

I shall try to send home some of the articles which we remove from the "Jerries," any quantity of helmets. I would like some of the things up in my room but still I don't know as I shall want to see anything after I get home to remind me of the war.

I did have a wonderful time in Paris but have been on the move since I left. I found a good bunch of letters when I rejoined the company.

Young Vanderbilt whose picture you sent, was one of the fifteen of us who came over in the advance party. He must have a pretty soft job now.

The clipping which you sent of the Reily boys from Syracuse who met in France I read with much interest. Young Reily and I were at the same school: he told me about meeting his brother who is in the draft army. The description of his brother was quite amusing.

Since returning from machine gun school I have little to do with gas work as most of my time is taken up handling a platoon which consists of four squads. But out of the lines I have charge of gas instruction, inspections, etc.

We expected to push on a little further today but since I started the letter we have received word we may stay here for the night so we have dug in and hoping to remain for a few hours.

The artillery all around us has started in again and believe me they are bumping some. No doubt old Jerry will be sending some back pretty quick.

Well we remained here for the night and may not move forward till this afternoon. The Chaplin held services this morning as it is Sunday, I took communion. It seems queer to hold services with each man carrying a gun. Reminds one of the Pilgrim days.

I may not get another chance to write again for a little while.[74]

Moran was killed in action. A letter written by Henry Cutter of the 105th Machine Gun Battery in December 1918 explained Moran's death as follows:

We were in the Hindenburg Stunt. One Sept. 27th another Sept. 29th at which time I was "lucky" and got out with nothing more than a broken or fractured radius bone, right forearm. Art at the time was still at a machine gun school, but reported back for duty the second week in Oct.

The line having been broken the machine gunners followed up the infantry until the next strong line of resistance, this was Oct. 17. He was a Sergeant in charge of a section and was leading forward his gun squads up a sunken road in the early morning when all of a sudden a shell landed on the road and then he met his fate. He suffered no pain whatever which may be some consolation.

Art was very popular and he was one of the many heroes who paid the supreme toll, in order that Humanity could be free from the Hun and Right should rule. Everyone laments over his fate and the Lord knows that no one does any more than I. Rooming with him I perhaps know him best of any fellow. Have always admired him for he was a man throughout and had a very high sense of duty as a soldier he was fearless and was looked up to and respected by all.

Memorial services were held for him and fellow comrades. His remains were buried in a nice grave at the head of which is a little wooden cross. The place of burial was near Bohain and Busiggney near Berguignette Farm. The graves are kept in fine condition and bodies will be transferred back to the states in due time.[75]

Harold LeRoy Naughton

Birth: October 22, 1889, Carbondale, Pennsylvania[76]
Death: October 17, 1918, France
Burial: Meuse-Argonne American Cemetery & Memorial, France; Memorial at Brookside Cemetery, Watertown, New York

Harold Naughton graduated from Watertown High School and entered Colgate University, which he attended for about two years.[77] He then entered New York Law School and, upon graduation, took up the practice of law in Watertown. On November 9, 1917, he married Miss Helen Aurilla Eager. Naughton entered Madison Barracks for officer training in May 1918 and was commissioned a captain in Company L of the 309th Infantry at Camp Dix in August 1917. He was sent overseas in May 1918. A letter from Major Henry Wilder explained the circumstances of Harold's death during the Battle of Argonne Forest:

The first night in the Argonne, October 16, on our trip to a new position across the forest I passed in the dim light of the early night endless truckloads of the wounded. I stopped several and finally located the trucks carrying the wounded from Harold's company. The men were almost too weak to talk, but I managed to find a few who told me and told me with great pride that Harold was in the thick of it that day—the first day I believe—and that he had luckily escaped a hit. But, they told me that his company was sadly shot up, having been given a particularly tough job against a strong line of machine guns and enemy artillery. But, the company had done its work well and were getting organized then for the next day's work.

That nights procession of wounded was something never to be forgotten and up to that night the neighboring division had last nearly half its men.

During the fighting that ensued to the right of Gran Pre—the toughest hell-hole in all of the Argonne—my own battalion of heavy howitzers of 809 F.A. was supporting Harold's regiment. Earlier we had been working for the 311th and 312th, but the last few days before Harold was evacuated we were given his regiment to back up. Up to this time I learned by telephone and from neighboring officers that Harold was surviving those stormy days all right, but that the remainder of his company was suffering heavily.

His company was attacking the Bois de Loges, a small woods on a hilltop, bristling with machine gun in impregnable holes and 77s and accurate snipers. He was up against a terrible proposition. This wood overlooked Grand Pre and from it the Boche raked the Grand Pre pocket night and day. Men and officers wounded near Grand Pre laid out exposed for as long as 14 days in some cases. I helped carry in a sergeant who was there 14 days. Harold was evacuated without delay however, if you can picture the worse possible military position for an attack, you have this spot. The Bois de Loges was taken, lost and retaken by our infantry seven times.

My battalion expended unlimited ammunition in the Bois de Loges region, dropping our 90 pound high explosives on those machine gun nests day after day and yet the Boche would again emerge from his caves with his machine guns. I believe that the Hun showed his stiffest fight in these woods. It was great personal satisfaction to have pounded and blasted those nests so much just at the time Harold was having his biggest fight, laying in miserable weather, never under cover with little food and with few men.

The personal discomforts of our infantry officers and men in this fight were indescribable. I believe that the 309th Heavy Artillery was able to reduce the infantry casualties and did render effective aid during those trying days. I was afraid Harold could not last against such resistance with his company attacking almost daily because I knew that his brigade was slowly wasting away, the losses in officers being the most severe. Our officers in those attacks always led and were always in the hottest spots, always disregarding danger.

First Lieutenant James Leo Mason of Gouverneur, an officer I recommended for the highest type of hero, was one of the first to get into the Bois de Loges on Nov. 1, in the final great attack and he reported that the heroism of our infantry was wonderful and that the havoc wrought by our heavy shells had been terrible.

The ground was utterly blown to pieces and yet always some enemy machine gunners remained to come up and fire. His observations does establish that our guns rendered the maximum assistance to the exhausted infantry who were fast wasting away in the supreme effort against the Bois de Loges.

One day they told me that Harold had been hit several times, but that they thought he surely would pull through. The next thing I heard the sad news from home.

Those who did not go through that Grand Pre fight will never know what our infantry contended with. Every artilleryman lost his heart to the poor infantrymen who suffered so much and faced such powerful enemy fire. To have made the supreme sacrifice under those conditions when regiments were reduced to one-sixth their strength is indeed a glorious opportunity. To lose such men is the greatest regret of the war, yet to have died on French soil is a hero's finest death after displaying such extraordinary heroism.[78]

Glenn N. Satterlee

Birth: March 31, 1892, Kalamazoo, Michigan
Death: August 1, 1918, France
Burial: Woodlawn Cemetery, Hamilton, New York

Glenn Satterlee moved to Brookfield with his family in 1898.[79] They moved to Hubbardsville one year later. While working on the farm of some of his relatives in Michigan, he decided to enlist during the summer of 1917. He joined Company C of the 126th Infantry and trained in Camp Gratin in Michigan, Camp MacArthur in Texas and Camp Merritt in New Jersey. He was in a field hospital, sick with the mumps, when his company originally left for France in March 1918. By April 1918, he was in France; he wrote to his mother:[80]

> *I will try and write a few lines to let you know that I am well and happy and I am in France where I have longed to be for some time.*
>
> *I am not with my own company yet and may never be with them again but you can just bet I will soldier just the same, I am with Company C of the 128th Infantry. Just at present they are going to try and get us back with our own after a while.*

Satterlee was killed in action in France.

LENOX

Luther Connell

Birth: Around 1898, Canastota, New York[81]
Death: October 5, 1918, France
Burial: Mount Pleasant Cemetery, Port Byron, New York

Luther Connell enlisted as a private into Company I of the 23rd Infantry on July 19, 1917. He was sent overseas on September 5, 1918, and he fought in the Battle of Soissons, the Battle of Saint-Mihiel and the Battle of Champagne. He wrote to his mother that he had

> *been over the top three times lately and has accounted for some Huns and best of all he has come out of the din of battle without a scratch. I am still in good health except for a French cold, which I have had ever since I got here, and do not seem able to get rid of. I don't mind the singing of the shells or the whistle of the bullets, so you see I am a veteran.*[82]

Connell was wounded on October 4, 1918, and died a day later.

Carl L. Foote

Birth: January 12, 1897,[83] Canastota, New York[84]
Death: June 23, 1918, France
Burial: Aisne Marne American Cemetery and Memorial, France

Prior to the war, Foote was working as a painter.[85] He enlisted as a private in June 1917. He was promoted to corporal in July 1917 and appears to have been demoted in January 1918 before being promoted to private first class in April 1918. He was killed in action at the Château-Thierry, France.[86] Private Edmond Mathieu wrote about Foote's death:

> *I belonged to the same company, E, "Fighting Ninth." I am sorry to say that I do know all about him for he was my pal. Pardon me if I hurt your feelings but it certainly is true that he was killed. My dear lady you have not heard from him since June because we were fighting hard at the time—all the month. Just as we were coming out of the trenches Carl forgot something and had to go back. As he did so he got shot by a German soldier. He was shot in the head and probably died instantly. He died game, as did many of the other boys. There are few of our company left—only a little bunch of twenty of us. Believe me we had some hard times. But God was with us and we knew it. Do not feel bad, because it cannot be helped. He has done his bit.*[87]

Eliphalet Houghton

Birth: November 26, 1895, Canastota, New York[88]
Death: September 17, 1919, France
Burial: Lenox Rural Cemetery, Canastota, New York

Prior to the war, Eliphalet Houghton attended Tri-State College in Angola, Indiana. He served in the Indiana National Guard, and on October 19, 1913, he married Letha E. Higbie in Angola. Letha died on October 23, 1918, in Michigan of pneumonia.[89] Eliphalet was inducted as a private into Company D of the 25th Engineers on September 25, 1917, training at Camp Dix in New Jersey.[90] He was promoted to private first class in April 1919. Houghton was sent overseas in February 1918. He referenced in letters being near the action during the war. Following the armistice, he took classes at a special technical school in Paris, and he worked on an electrical crew. Houghton was killed in an electrocution accident.

Carlton A. Lower

Birth: July 19, 1899, Newark, New Jersey[91]
Death: September 28, 1918, France
Death: Meuse-Argonne American Cemetery & Memorial, France

Carlton Lower's mother died at a young age, and his aunt and uncle, Mr. and Mrs. Claude Jackson of Canastota, raised him. Lower graduated from Canastota High School in the spring of 1917. He enlisted as a private in the First Battery of the Field Artillery on August 19, 1917.[92] Lower earned promotions to private first class in December 1917 and corporal in July 1918. He was sent overseas in December 1917. He transferred to the 301st Tank Company in June 1918. He was killed in action in France.

Charles M. Miller

Birth: March 14, 1898, Canastota, New York[93]
Death: July 15, 1918, France
Burial: Lenox Rural Cemetery, Canastota, New York

Charles Miller grew up in Canastota, living with his paternal grandparents following the death of his parents at a young age.[94] He was working at a gun plant in Ithaca when he enlisted as a private in the army on September 13, 1917.[95] Miller was assigned to Company L of the 30th Infantry and trained at Camp Dix. He went overseas on April 2, 1918. Miller was killed in action when a shell struck him as the Allies made their first push near Château-Thierry, France.

Joel N. Waterbury

Birth: November 26, 1891, Canastota, New York[96]
Death: February 9, 1919, France
Burial: Suresnes American Cemetery and Memorial, France

Prior to the war, Joel Waterbury was living with his parents and working on their farm. He was inducted as a private into the second company of the 1st Training Battalion on September 29, 1917.[97] He was assigned to Camp Dix in New Jersey and later Camp Gordon in Georgia for training. He was transferred to Company G of the 325th Infantry in March 1918. Waterbury was sent overseas in April 1918 and fought in the Battle of Argonne Forest. He died of pulmonary tuberculosis.

George H. Wilson

Birth: September 6, 1892, Canastota, New York[98]
Death: January 9, 1919, Camp McClellan, Alabama
Burial: Mount Pleasant Cemetery, Canastota, New York

Prior to the war, George Wilson was working as a teamster.[99] He was inducted as a private into the Headquarters Company of the 34th Field Artillery on August 8, 1918. He was stationed at Camp McClellan in Alabama. Wilson transferred to the Supply Company of the 34th Field Artillery and was promoted to wagoner around November 1918. He died of pneumonia at the Base Hospital at Camp McClellan.

LINCOLN

Nicholas Gregg

Birth: April 18, 1890, Merrillsville, New York[100]
Death: November 1, 1918, France[101]
Burial: Perryville Cemetery, Fenner, New York

Prior to the war, Nicholas Gregg was working as a carpenter.[102] He was inducted as a private into Company G of the 311th Infantry on April 19, 1918. He was assigned to Camp Dix in New Jersey before being transported overseas in May 1918. Gregg was wounded in action on September 21, 1918. Gregg was killed in action at Grand Pre in the Argonne Forest.[103] His remains were returned home in September 1921.

MADISON

Stephen John Downey

Birth: 1898, Utica, New York[104]
Death: November 24, 1917, Off the Coast of Spain
Burial: Memorialized on the Tablet of the Missing in Surrey, England; Monument at St. Bernard's Cemetery, Waterville, New York

Stephen Downey grew up in Bouckville working at Dr. C.M. Coe's general store. In the fall of 1916, he moved to Schenectady to accept a job with the electric works.[105] He joined the navy in April 1917.[106] He was assigned to the Naval Training Station in Newport, Rhode Island, where he obtained the rank of seaman second class. He served for three months on the USS *Maine* before being transferred to draft detail in New York City. In October 1917, he was assigned to the USS *Actaeon*, a merchant ship, as a gunner. He wrote to his cousin J. Frank Downey about his experiences on October 6, 1917:

> *I thought I had better celebrate my return to the states by writing home to let you know I am on deck and going strong. I don't wonder that you think I have been sunk because I didn't write, but I have been in the US only about a week in the last three months. I was transferred to the Cruiser Des Moines from the Maine in July, as a signalman for convoy duty, and I left on her and went to Sydney, Cape Breton Island, where we joined 14 merchant ships and escorted them to within 100 miles of Ireland and there we met some American destroyers which took them the rest of the way in and we*

came back to New York. Well, we hadn't any more than dropped anchor in New York when I was transferred to the Albany and from the Albany to the Idomencus an English ship of the Alfred Hold line, and with 11 other merchant ships and the Albany for an escort, we started across again. About six days out from New York we ran into the worst hurricane the officers said they ever saw. We had a gale blowing about 120 miles per hour. Rather a strong breeze! The sea ran mountain high. I think that at least the waves were a hundred feet high because they washed over the bridge.

Just as I was going on watch at 12 o'clock that night a big wave carried me from one side of the deck to the other and wrapped me around the iron rail. It laid me up for three days in bed, with a strained side and a bad cold. The next morning it calmed down quite a lot and we found all our ships but two, one of which got to Ireland. The other we never heard from again.[107]

Stephen received a commendation for bravery when a ship he was on, the *Magnolia*, was torpedoed. Serving as a gunner, he was commended for saving the lives of four of his comrades.[108] He wrote about those experiences in the letter to J. Frank Downey:

Well I had been around on deck again about four days and was down in my room at 3:10 in the afternoon, when all of a sudden I heard a terrible explosion, and was picked up and thrown about 15 feet through a door and then I knew that we were torpedoed and also found out that there was a war on. Well, to make a long story short we lost only six men killed and they were down below in the engine rooms where the torpedo came in. The rest of the crew abandoned the ship, only 13 of us and we got things from Ireland and ran the ship ashore on Barra Head. It is an island in the Hebrides group, west of Scotland. We salvaged the ship. We were taken by a British Destroyer to Lough Swilley, a little town in County Donegal, and there were given transportation to Liverpool, England. We went by train to Belfast by way of Londonderry and I had a ride on a jaunting car across the city of Liverpool, arriving there on a Thursday, and left on the steamship Baltic for New York: and believe me, the most cheerful sight I saw in a long time was the Statue of Liberty as we came up the bay. Well, glad they didn't sink me this time, and I don't believe there is a German that can.

If I get paid on the 20th I am going to put in a request for 10 days leave to come home.[109]

On November 24, 1917, Downey's ship was torpedoed for a second time off the coast of Spain, and he died during the attack. Downey's remains were lost at sea.

Lynn E. Kelly

Birth: February 26, 1891, Bouckville, New York[110]
Death: August 17, 1918, France[111]
Burial: Flanders Field American Cemetery and Memorial, Belgium

Prior to the war, Lynn Kelly was working as a knitter at the Augusta Knitting Company in Utica. He moved to Waterville and later Utica. He was inducted as a private in the National Guard on July 23, 1917.[112] He was sent overseas in May 1918 and promoted to private first class in August of the same year. Not long after his promotion, he was killed in action.

NELSON

Louis F. Kelsey

Birth: March 31, 1888, Chichester, New York[113]
Death: January 13, 1919, New York, New York
Burial: Oak Grove Cemetery, Burlington, Pennsylvania

Louis Kelsey was ordained a minister in 1909 and was assigned to the Nelson-Erieville charge in October 1910, serving four years in Madison County.[114] He married Mary E. Ross on August 11, 1909, in Elmira, New York.[115] They had two daughters, Mable (1911) and Ruthadel (1912), and one son, Louis (1919). While in Nelson, he attended Cazenovia Seminary, graduating in 1914 as the president of the class. In October 1914, he was transferred to Cicero, New York, where he continued his studies at Syracuse University, graduating in 1917. Following his graduation, Kelsey was commissioned a first lieutenant and chaplain on July 5, 1918. He was assigned to Camp Taylor in Kentucky before being sent overseas in July 1918. He was wounded while overseas. He wrote home to his wife about his treatment:

> *The Red Cross is doing fine work here. Do all you can for the Red Cross. I have had a chance to wear a few of the bandages. At the present time I am bound up in them, and I often wonder whether they were made in Cicero. Anyway the thought makes me feel better.*
>
> *We are much encouraged by the way the war is going. The American Army is getting organized and when it is the Boche is going to h--l where*

he belongs. The people in the States only know one quarter of the things that are going on.[116]

Kelsey returned to a hospital in New York City in October 1918, suffering from a "severe case of shell shock." He returned home twice while being treated. Kelsey's cause of death has conflicting reports. Kelsey's service card claims that he died because of suicide from jumping out of a window. Newspaper reports have him dying from pneumonia. In the summer of 1919, Mrs. Kelsey gave birth to a son, Louis F. Kelsey Jr.[117]

ONEIDA

Earl Alger

Birth: March 23, 1893, Martinsburg, New York[118]
Death: October 18, 1918, France
Burial: Martinsburg Cemetery, New York

Earl Alger grew up in Martinsburg, New York, before moving to Oneida Castle around 1916.[119] He was working as a farmer, likely on the family farm. Alger was inducted as a private into Company B of the 310th Infantry on September 28, 1917. Alger trained at Camp Dix (New Jersey). He was promoted to private first class in February 1918. He was sent overseas in May 1918. He was killed after being struck by shrapnel in the Argonne Forest.

Herbert Lyle Armstrong

Birth: November 11, 1888, Rome, New York[120]
Death: September 29, 1918, France
Burial: Rome Cemetery, New York

Herbert Lyle Armstrong attended schools in Rome and briefly worked at Rome Wire Company. Around 1910, he moved to Albion, New York, to work with the Burt Olney Canning Company. He later moved to Oneida and continued to work for the canning company as a traveling salesman and later as a bookkeeper.[121] Armstrong was inducted as a private in Company E of the 59th Infantry on February 22, 1918.[122] He was then assigned to Camp Devens in Massachusetts and later Camp Mills in New York. Armstrong served in the Intelligence Corps. In this post, he was placed in charge of listening posts in the front line of the trenches, patrol duty and sniping. He was sent overseas in May 1918. He fought in the Marne and Argonne Campaigns, as well as at Saint-Mihiel. He was killed in action.

Calvin Wells Cochran

Birth: February 9, 1895, Oneida Castle, New York[123]
Death: August 10, 1918, France
Burial: Glenwood Cemetery, Oneida, New York

Calvin Wells Cochran graduated from Oneida High School and attended Colgate University as part of the class of 1919.[124] He was a member of the Sigma Alpha (later Phi Delta Theta) fraternity and a member of the Chemical Society. He joined the army as a private on February 22, 1918, and was assigned to Camp Devens.[125] He transferred to Camp Mills, where he was assigned to the Machine Gun Company of the 59th Infantry. Cochran left for France on May 1. He fought in the battle at Château-Thierry in mid-July and the drive for Picardy in August. He was killed in action. In February 1920, the Cochran Memorial Church in Oneida Castle built an addition, which was dedicated as the Wells Cochran Memorial Chapel.

Percy Ayers Dean

Birth: August 22, 1897, Oneida, New York[126]
Death: October 7, 1918, France[127]
Burial: Glenwood Cemetery, Oneida, New York

Prior to the war, Percy Dean was working as a laborer at the pulley company.[128] He enlisted as a private in Company I of the 22nd Infantry on May 1, 1917. Dean was assigned to Fort Hamilton, where he trained for three months. He was sent overseas in August 1917. He served in General Pershing's headquarters for six months before being promoted to corporal in February 1918. Following his promotion, Dean was transferred to Company L

of the 26th Infantry. While overseas, he served in the Marne, Saint-Mihiel and Argonne Forest. He was wounded in his hand in July 1918. Following the injury, he wrote to his father:

> *I have got a good souvenir I would like to send home but I am afraid it will get lost. It's an Iron Cross and believe me I had to fight for it, too. I was offered 100 francs (that's pretty near $100), but I guess I will keep it. Don't worry about me because I am lively and full of fight as ever. It certainly was some sight to see the boys walk right into machine gun bullets and shrapnel and kill and capture the whole bunch; send those that were able on back, and keep right on the next objective. My belief is that this war won't take over three months longer. The Boche don't want to see any more Americans up in front of them because we certainly gave them a run for their lives. I did my share and feel satisfied. The Red Cross and YMCA help carry in the wounded and have hot drinks and cakes back of the lines. I won't say anymore as I want this letter to go through.*

Dean was killed in action during the Meuse-Argonne Campaign in France. On December 21, 1920, Dean was posthumously awarded the New York Conspicuous Service Star. His remains were returned home in October 1921.[129]

James Bernard Dunn

Birth: January 6, 1889, Oneida, New York[130]
Death: September 5, 1918, France
Burial: Oisne-Aisne American Cemetery and Memorial, France

Prior to the war, James Bernard Dunn was working as a watchman at the railroad[131] and a painter.[132] He was engaged to Miss T. Bella Jennings.[133] At the outbreak of the war, Dunn attempted to enlist but was rejected due to his short stature.[134] He was drafted on February 22, 1918, and trained at Camp Devens in Massachusetts. In a letter to Jennings, he wrote that he was

> *on the firing line where he had been in action for 61 days. He had been notified that he would be sent to a rest billet about September 15.*

He was killed in action in France.

Cecil T. Ernenwein

Birth: July 27, 1892, Oneida, New York[135]
Death: January 13, 1918, Washington State
Burial: Stockbridge Cemetery, New York

Around 1903, Cecil Ernenwein's family moved to Lake Placid.[136] Prior to the war, he was working as a printer while still living with his family. He enlisted in the U.S. Army Corps of Engineers in December 1917. Ernenwein died of diphtheria at the Vancouver Barracks.[137] Following his death, his mother received a letter from Cecil explaining military life:

> *Though I have not yet received any mail from you, I know it must be on the way or held up at Fort Slocum. I am particularly anxious to know whether my suitcase arrived OK.*
>
> *These Barracks are the finest in the USA and the officers are the finest lot of gentleman I have yet met in the army. We get all the good, wholesome, clean food we want. After my siege at Fort Slocum it seems like coming back home. As long as I remain here I am happy. I went to the First Church in Portland this morning, then had a good chicken dinner as on that day I stood out in the snow and sleet before daylight, 4 AM at Fort Slocum, until we were all packed into the transports and run down along the Atlantic coast to New York. There we did a bit of marching around the city and after waiting several hours they packed us into a train—300 of us—all engineers.*
>
> *I think I should have been sent to Washington, DC instead of the State of Washington, but after you stand on the bridge and say "I do" you go where they send you. About 4 PM they came through with boxes of sandwiches, etc. We were all pretty tired the first night, as there was a lot of supplies to load and reload on both boat and train. We finally struck Utica in the West Shore late at night, passed through Syracuse while asleep and was just awake when we struck Rochester.*
>
> *We crossed into Canada at Niagara Falls late that second afternoon or on the 26th. I was awake lots of the time as I had not yet got used to the congested condition. We crossed the border or rather, went under it at Port Huron on the 27th about 7 AM.*

Martin Girolamo

Birth: January 9, 1893, Alberobello, Italy[138]
Death: May 12, 1918, France
Burial: Unknown

Martin Girolamo arrived in the United States in March 1910.[139] He married Catherine Doria on May 15, 1915.[140] Unfortunately, she died less than a year later, on March 6, 1916, and is buried at St. Patrick's Cemetery in Oneida.[141] Prior to enlisting, Martin was working for the New York Central Railroad. He enlisted in June 1917 as a private in the army, serving in the infantry. Martin Girolamo (also spelled "Geralamo") became the first Oneida resident to die in France when he died of wounds he received in battle.

Elon E. Hill

Birth: June 11, 1893, Utica, New York[142]
Death: September 16, 1918, France
Burial: Glenwood Cemetery, Oneida, New York

Before the war, Elon Hill was working as a filer at the steel pulley factory,[143] as a laborer for an ice company[144] and at Oneida Limited soldering silver.[145] Prior to the war, he married Reta Parkhust. They had one son, Vernie, born in September 1916. Elon was inducted into the army as a private in Company B of the 310th Infantry on September 28, 1917. He was later transferred to the Headquarters Company of the 60th Infantry. He was sent overseas in April 1918. He wrote his family in late August that he

> *had been over the top three times and was leaving the trenches after 14 straight days of fighting for a rest camp.*[146]

Hill was killed in action. Following his death, Hill's captain, Duff G. Phillips, wrote to his mother:

It is indeed with a heavy heart that I answer your letter of November 10th. I wish I could tell you otherwise, but I cannot, for I know positively that he is dead, died on the field of battle, fighting for the cause of right, which has prevailed through the death of noble sons like yours. He was indeed a fine boy, one any mother would be proud of, a soldier we were all proud of.

On September 16th in the battle of St. Mihiel he was killed and we buried him near the spot where he fell. His grave was marked and the proper person has that location of that if his folk's desire and the government so decides on that course, his body can be taken home.

My heart almost breaks as I think of you and your grief. I have a mother who has waited and watched just as you have, and I have often thought about how she would feel if such news came to you should have gone to her. I am a father and have a son 18 years old. May God alone, who you can comfort at such times, bring you relief. Your son died a soldier's death, loved by all who knew him.[147]

ELLIOT P. HINDS

Birth: September 14, 1873, Oneida, New York[148]
Death: June 24, 1918, France
Burial: Oneida Community Cemetery, Oneida, New York

Elliot Hinds was raised in the Oneida Community until it was disbanded. He received a scholarship and attended Cornell University, earning a mechanical engineering degree in 1896. He moved to Niagara Falls, where he was the manager of the Hinds Paper Box Works, after the death of his father in 1910. In 1904, he married Marie Oswald. They had two children: daughter Evelyn and son William.[149] Elliot was also a very well-respected tennis player. Hinds was called into service on July 20, 1917, and commissioned as a first lieutenant in the aviation section of the Signals Corps in San Diego, California.[150] He was an instructor in Tennessee and Illinois. He was commissioned a captain and placed in charge of the third detachment of flying cadets in France. Following their training, Hinds was placed in active duty. He was credited with training several prominent pilots. He served as the commanding officer of the 12th Aero Squadron, as well as flight commander. He was also one of the oldest pilots in the service at the age of forty-four. Hinds died when his plane crashed in Colombey-les-Belles,

France. His family received a letter following his death noting that he had been forced to stay behind due to defective parts; whether or not this played a role in his death is unknown.

Sheldon Clarke Houston

Birth: January 3, 1889, Lowell, Massachusetts[151]
Death: November 3, 1918, France
Burial: Green-Wood Cemetery, Brooklyn, New York

Sheldon Houston lived in Oneida Castle with the family of Clarence Klock and was a member of St. John's Episcopal Church in Oneida.[152] Prior to the war, Houston was working in Haworth, New Jersey, as an inspector for ABC lights.[153] Houston was a corporal in Company H of the 310th Infantry. In a letter, Captain Sterling Gault explained the circumstances of Houston's death:

> *Corporal Sheldon C. Houston was killed in action on the afternoon of November 3rd, 1918: on that day he was advancing with his company in the Bois des Petises Armoises about fifty kilometers north of Grand Pre. The company was held up in the woods by strong enemy machine gun positions.*
>
> *Late in the afternoon while, moving about in the woods with his squad Corporal Houston was struck near the heart by a stray machine gun bullet. Though conscious for some time after receiving the wound, he died within an hour.*

Claude R. Johnston

Birth: Around 1897[154]
Death: October 22, 1918, England
Burial: Glenwood Cemetery, Oneida, New York

Claude Johnston graduated from Oneida High School and was a popular musician in the area.[155] He enlisted as a landsman for machinist's mate in the aviation section of the navy on January 26, 1918. He trained in Charleston, South Carolina; Pensacola, Florida; and Philadelphia,

Pennsylvania, before serving overseas at a naval station in Killingholme, England. He was promoted to landsman for quartermaster in July 1918 and quartermaster second class in November 1918. According to a burial notice, he served in the hydroplane service, and his brother Clarence served in the navy.[156] He died from pneumonia.[157]

DANIEL H. KINNEY

Birth: January 1, 1889, Florence, New York[158]
Death: February 12, 1919, France
Burial: Semur, France

Prior to the war, Daniel Kinney was working as a bartender at the St. James Hotel in Oneida. He was inducted as a private into Company G of the 311th Infantry April 1918 and was assigned to Camp Dix.[159] He was sent overseas in May 1918 and took part in the Saint-Mihiel and Meuse-Argonne Offensives. In a letter home to Kinney's sister from Private George Brown, he wrote about Dan's experiences and illness overseas:

> *Dan and I have been always together since the date that Dan arrived in France or for a period of nine months. Dan did not enjoy the best of health, particularly during the times we were in action. However, he did not complain much and at all times performed his duties as if he was in the best of health, thereby being loyal to his superiors and country, showing or rather proving himself to be a true soldier. But I am coming to a very unpleasant task which is telling you of Dan's sickness.*
>
> *Dan was taken ill on February 8 with the flu and sent to the hospital at Semur, remaining there but four days and he was called to his reward February 12, Lincoln's birthday. After arriving at the hospital he soon contracted pneumonia and died on the morning of the 12th.*
>
> *He was buried in the little cemetery at Semur on February 13. A burial detail of fifteen soldiers accompanied the body and were present at the services. The pall bearers were lads of Company G, and included the only two of the twenty-six Oneida Boys who departed on that date, while the*

firing squad was composed of Dan's friends from the Supply Company, to which he was last attached.

The three Oneida boys who acted as pall bearers were Lee Davis of Munnsville, Guy Brophy of Canastota and myself. Dan was accorded a military funeral with all the honors of the army. A firing squad, a volley of shots over his grave, while the bugler sounded taps. The Catholic chaplain was present and delivered a very impressive sermon.

The captain of our company had given me permission to open Dan's three letters and that is how I happened to be answering this letter. However, you may learn of Dan's death long before this letter reaches you as no doubt Dan's parents have received official notice from Washington.

Dan was always wishing for that great day of departure for the States to see his friends again and I'm sure that Dan would not want to have the answer to your letter delayed, so I have taken the liberty of answering.

Dan was held in high esteem by the boys of company G, as well as the lads of the Supply company and words are too feeble to express the deep sympathy which I hold, for it was a terrible blow to have him taken from our midst, but as the saying is and always will be perhaps for best, "God's will be done, as He knows best." However I will say that Dan was well prepared to meet his maker.[160]

Ernest G. Koch

Birth: April 22, 1896, Syracuse, New York[161]
Death: September 26, 1918, France
Burial: Glenwood Cemetery, Oneida, New York

Prior to the war, Ernest Koch was working as the secretary of the Plumber's Union.[162] His brother Charles was a gunner on the USS *Arkansas*. Koch was inducted as a private into Company E of the 348th Infantry on May 25, 1918. He was transferred to the Medical Replacement Unit. He went overseas in early September 1918, and upon his arrival, he was taken directly from his transport ship to a hospital after contracting pneumonia. A commander from the hospital wrote to Koch's mother:

It is with very deep regret that I have to inform you of the death of your son, Ernest G. Koch, private, US Army. He was admitted to the hospital direct from a US transport suffering from pneumonia in an advanced stage. As you no doubt know this disease pursues its course very rapidly and although every known treatment was given, he died on September 26, 1918, one day after admission.

Your son was held in very high esteem by the men of his unit and I must say that a man of his character an ability is a severe loss to our country at this time, when valuable men are so badly needed.

He was buried in our military cemetery (Kerfautras), Brest, France.

Lawrence (Laurence) Uebelacker

Birth: 1898, Canastota, New York[163]
Death: September 29, 1918, France
Burial: Glenwood Cemetery, Oneida, New York

Lawrence Uebelacker enlisted in the 3rd Infantry of the New York National Guard (later Company F of the 108th Infantry) on June 27, 1917. He went overseas in May 1918. He was killed in action on September 29, 1918, during an attack on the famed German Hindenburg Line in France. Lieutenant Gurney Wilder spoke about Uebelacker in Oneida in December 1918:

> *I have the greatest admiration for one of your young men. I think he had the finest character and the greatest backbone and grit of any fellow I ever saw, and his bravery was far beyond the average. He gave his life fighting for what he thought was right. He was a hero of whom you may well be proud.*

Wilder spoke of the day that Uebelacker died:

> *The 108th was given the task of capturing the strongest point in the Hindenburg line, which five army corps had failed to take in five previous attempts. The "line" was an almost solid mass of barbed wire about a quarter of a mile through and stretching for miles.*
>
> *The plan was to go over at 4:30 o'clock in the morning. The American artillery drenched the German areas for several hours with a terrible barrage, to which the enemy replied with gas shells for a number of hours also. With scarcely anything but shell holes for protection, none of the men in Co. F were killed during this bombardment, although a few were injured.*
>
> *Four-thirty arrived and the first wave of 108th men went over the top for the attack, following behind their own barrage. Just as the second wave*

started after them, the Germans lowered their barrage and caught the men as they were leaving the trenches. The casualties were very severe and how the men survived was a miracle. Nevertheless, many of them went on through the hail of machine gun bullets and the bursting shells. They gained their objectives but at a great price. The Australian troops, which followed them in the third wave, relieved the men of the 108th and held the positions, which the 108th had captured.

Wilder quoted Field Marshal Haigh, who said later:

Never in all my experience have I seen so many dead Germans in one spot as this.

He finished with a review of the men of Company F:

There were no better men in my command than the Oneida boys; there were no better soldiers than your sons. Standing in the trenches to their knees in the mud or mire with the rain soaking them to the hide they never grumbled. They were playing a man's game in a man's way.

SMITHFIELD

Asa C. Vedder

Birth: September 6, 1893, Lenox, New York[164]
Death: August 22, 1918, France
Burial: Glenwood Cemetery Oneida, New York

Prior to the war, Asa Vedder was working on the family farm in Smithfield.[165] He was drafted and inducted as a private in Company L of the 305th Infantry in February 1918.[166] He trained at Camp Devens in Massachusetts. He went overseas in April 1918. He was the only known Madison County resident to die after being exposed to gas. A letter from Susie L. Dyer, who was part of the Home Communication Service for the Red Cross at U.S. Base Hospital 19 in Vichy, explained what happened:

> *As the representative of the Home Communication Service of the American Red Cross it becomes my sad duty to give you such information as I can concerning the death of Pvt. Asa Vedder which took place at this hospital at 6:30 am on August 22, 1918. It was caused by the absorption of deleterious gas by inhalation and surface contact received in action August 16th. He was transferred to this hospital from a hospital nearer the front on August 18th. May it be of some comfort to you to know that he received the*

best of care from our nurses and doctors, who did everything that they could to save his life and make him comfortable.

He was given a military funeral with an escort of American and French soldiers. One of his comrades was buried at the same time and their caskets were covered with the flags of two countries. They were laid to rest in the lovely little cemetery on the edge of the town. It is in a lovely spot from which one looks across the valley to the beautiful surrounding hills.

We of the Red Cross extend to you our deepest sympathy. It is a great privilege and honor for us to do what little we can for our brave boys.[167]

STOCKBRIDGE

Samuel Arthur Bovee

Birth: July 3, 1901, Hepburnville, Pennsylvania[168]
Death: July 26, 1918, France
Burial: Stockbridge Cemetery, New York

Samuel Bovee enlisted in the Marine Corps as a private on November 7, 1916.[169] He trained in Port Royal, South Carolina, and Quantico, Virginia. He was promoted to corporal on June 8, 1917. Bovee was transported overseas in June 1917. He was a member of the 61st Company, 1st Battalion, and 5th Regiment. Bovee was wounded in France on July 19, 1918, and taken to a hospital near the village of Ognon, north of Paris, where he died a week later.

Wayne Jewell Buckman

Birth: December 20, 1891, Stockbridge[170]
Death: June 7, 1918, France
Burial: Hillside Cemetery, Clarendon, New York

At a young age, Wayne Jewell Buckman moved with his family to Holley, New York, where he went to school. He attended Louisiana State University and then moved to Flint, Michigan, where he worked as a landscaper prior to the war. He enlisted in the U.S. Marine Corps in August 1917. He trained at Parris Island, South Carolina, and Quantico, Virginia, until he was sent overseas in December 1917. In his last letter home, he wrote about the plants that he saw and his desire to beautify the family home upon his return. He also sent money for his parents to have a photo taken together to send to him. He was killed in action at Château-Thierry in France on June 7, 1918, and a letter sent to his parents by Major General George Barnett stated the following:

> *Deeply regret to inform you, cablegram from abroad states that Private Jewell Buckman, Marine Corps, was killed in action June 7. Remains will be interred abroad until the end of the war. Accept my heartfelt sympathy in your great loss. Your son nobly gave his life in service for his country.*

HORACE ELMER DAVENPORT

Birth: January 10, 1889, Munnsville, New York[171]
Death: September 24, 1918, France
Burial: Stockbridge Cemetery, New York

Prior to the war, Horace Davenport was working at the family farm,[172] and later he worked in Sherrill.[173] He was inducted as a private into Company B of the 310th Infantry on September 8, 1917.[174] Davenport was sent overseas in January 1918 and was transferred to the Headquarters Company of the 104th infantry in August 1918. Horace was killed in action on September 24, 1918, and is buried at Stockbridge Cemetery.

SULLIVAN

George H. Northing

Birth: August 24, 1896, Lincolnshire, England[175]
Death: October 16, 1918, France
Burial: Meuse-Argonne American Cemetery & Memorial, France

George H. Northing enlisted as a private in Company E of the 38th Infantry on August 17, 1917.[176] He was promoted to corporal in February 1918 and sent overseas the following month. He was seriously wounded in action on August 8, 1918, but was able to return.[177] Northing held an outpost near Thiaucourt for two weeks in late September 1918. He was killed in action while fighting during the advance near Champigneulles, France.

Claude Elmer Sayles

Birth: October 1889, Bridgeport, New York[178]
Death: June 6, 1918, France
Burial: Aisne-Marne American Cemetery, France

At a young age, Claude Sayles's family moved to Herkimer County[179] and later to Montgomery County.[180] Prior to the war, he was working as a farm laborer. He enlisted in the Marine Corps in April 1917. Following his initial training at Parris Island, he was shipped to France in June 1917. In a letter to his father shortly before his death, he noted:

> [I]*t was lots of fun up there to hear the big guns firing in front and behind us and the machine guns rattling and the big shells hummer over our heads. So you see it was very interesting.*[181]

He was killed in action during the Château-Thierry Offensive in France. Shortly before his death, he wrote a letter to his father:

> *I am still well and happy and hope you are the same.*
>
> *I suppose you get lots of news about the war and what the Americans are doing. We haven't had a death in our company yet. Only one or two have received wounds.*
>
> *Received the papers and, believe me, I was glad to get them. We were in the front line trenches at the time, but we are back in our rest billets now and it seems good. Sleeping in a fairly good bunk and sleeping in a dugout where the rats are as large as cats and the mice are as thick as flies around a honey pail are two different things.*
>
> *But it was lots of fun up there to hear the big guns firing in front and behind us, and the machine rattling and the big shells humming over our heads. So, you see, it was very interesting.*[182]

JOHN E. WHEELER

Birth: Around 1898, Chittenango Station, New York[183]
Death: October 8, 1918, France
Burial: Oakwood Cemetery, Chittenango, New York

John Wheeler's father died in 1906. Prior to the war, John was working as a farm laborer. He enlisted as a private in Company F of the 23rd Infantry. He was promoted to private first class in January 1918 and then corporal in October 1918. He was sent overseas in September 1917 and fought at the Battle of Champagne. He wrote to his mother about how he enjoyed France and the fellowship he felt with English and French soldiers.[184] He died of wounds received in action.

PART II

WORLD WAR II

On September 1, 1939, German troops invaded western Poland. Two days later, Britain and France declared war on Germany. On September 17, 1939, Soviet troops invaded eastern Poland. Poland quickly fell, and so started the Second World War. Germany invaded Norway, Belgium and the Netherlands and occupied Denmark before invading France in 1940. In June 1940, Italy formed an alliance with Germany and declared war against France and Britain. By mid-June, France had requested an armistice. Germany then turned its attention to Britain, which it bombed extensively for eight months from September 1940 until May 1941. While the United States stayed neutral during this time, it did approve the Lend-Lease Act, which stated that the government could lend or lease war supplies to any country that was deemed vital to the defense of the United States. This allowed the country to remain neutral while still helping its allies.

Japan began its imperial expansion in 1931 in Manchuria and continued its expansion throughout the decade before invading China in 1937. The Japanese quickly captured Beijing, Shanghai and Nanjing, which was the capital of China. The United States responded to the invasion of China with economic sanctions and trade embargoes. In September 1940, Japan signed the Tripartite Pact, in which the signatories each agreed to help each other if any of them were attacked by a country that was not currently in the war. Later in September, the Japanese occupied French Indochina. The United States placed additional economic sanctions on Japan, which included an embargo on oil and steel. A little over a year later, on December 7, 1941, Japan attacked the American base at Pearl Harbor in Hawaii. The attack took less than two hours, but it significantly damaged nearly twenty ships and more than three hundred airplanes. More than 2,400 individuals were killed in the attack, and nearly 1,000 people were injured. The following day, Congress approved President Franklin Roosevelt's declaration of war on Japan. On December 11, 1941, Germany and Italy declared war on the United States. The United States declared war on Germany and Italy on the same day.

Leading up to World War II, Madison County's population was nearly identical to the population in 1920, just after World War I ended. The Madison County Draft and Draft Board was reformed in September 1940.[185] Two districts oversaw the draft for the county. District 1 (Draft Board 440) covered the city of Oneida and the towns of Fenner, Lenox, Lincoln, Oneida, Smithfield, Stockbridge and Sullivan. District 2 (Draft Board 441) covered the towns of Brookfield, Cazenovia, DeRuyter, Eaton, Georgetown, Hamilton, Lebanon, Madison and Nelson. The three-man draft committee for District 1 consisted of Edwin P. Clay, an optometrist who served in the army; Stockbridge Valley Central School principal Alfred G. Zeller; and Oneida mayor Ansel K. Zellner.[186] The three-man draft committee for District 2 consisted of Isaiah M. Charlton, who was the former director of the New York State School of Agriculture in Morrisville; James Feeley, a banker in Hamilton; and World War I veteran Edward G.B. Fox of Cazenovia. The district had three advisory committee persons: Earl Armstrong, World War I veteran from Hamilton; Amos Fox, the treasurer of Madison County 4-F from DeRuyter; and Ten-Eyck Wendell of Cazenovia.

The Madison County War Loan Committee oversaw eight campaigns for raising funds. Madison County Highway superintendent Lynn E. Johnson oversaw a number of the campaigns and was replaced by David R.C. Smith of Canastota. The campaigns raised more than $15 million in funding.

Colgate University (as well as the University of Rochester and Cornell University) offered a V-12 Training program, which helped to generate officers for the navy and marines via completing a bachelor's

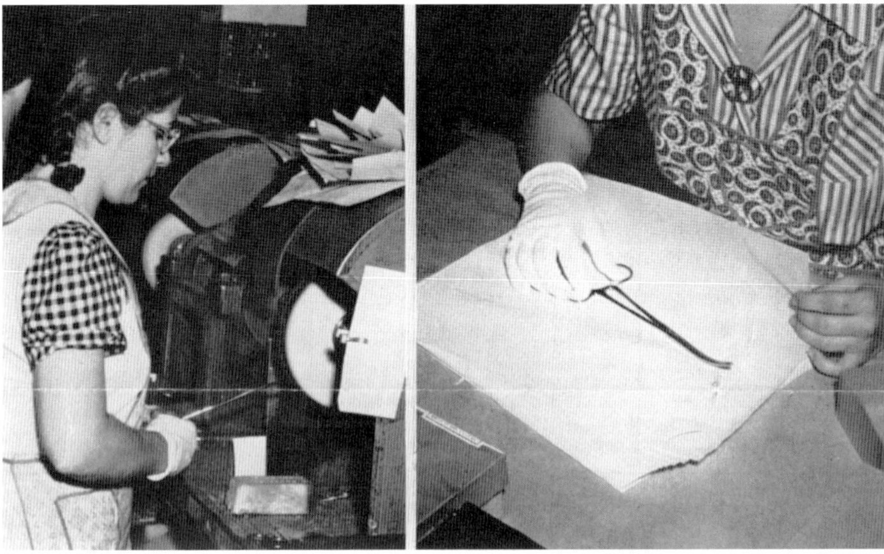

Oneida Community Limited Employees producing surgical forceps. Image taken from the *Kenwood Chronicle*. *Courtesy of the Oneida Community Mansion House.*

degree at the college and then attending specialized training. For the marines, the training was boot camp and officers' school; upon completion, they were commissioned second lieutenants. For the navy, the candidates would complete a Naval Reserve Midshipman's School. Upon graduation, the sailors were commissioned ensigns.

A number of industries converted to wartime production, most commonly in northern Madison County. Oneida Limited once again converted to producing materials, including silverware, surgical tools, rifle sights, parachute releases, hand grenades, shells, survival guns, bayonets, aircraft fuel tanks and chemical bombs. During the war, Oneida Limited purchased the Rex-Watson Company in Canastota to help meet demands. Oneida Limited completed more than $56 million in war contracts and received four Army-Navy "E" awards. The Westcott Chuck Company of Oneida converted to wartime production and made an "undisclosed part" that was used in the development of the atomic bomb in Oak Ridge, Tennessee.[187] The Company of Master Craftsmen in Oneida produced glider wings and furniture for naval ships.

Hugo Keller operated the Keller Motor Company. During the war, the inability to get vehicles forced him to turn his car company into something different.[188] He formed Keller Laboratories, where they designed a device that bandaged injured limbs. The company had twenty-three employees and was the smallest plant in the country to receive an Army-Navy "E" Award.

The images that appear in this section are courtesy of *A Book of Remembrance* unless otherwise noted.

BROOKFIELD

Norman W. Ballard

Birth: June 4, 1919, Cooperstown, New York[189]
Death: August 31, 1944, France
Burial: American Cemetery & Memorial, France; Memorialized at Evergreen Cemetery, Lee, New York

Norman Ballard grew up in Oneida County, but his family moved to Leonardsville sometime after his father's death in 1940. Prior to the war, he worked at Revere Copper & Brass in Rome, New York.[190] Ballard and his wife, Hazel, had a son, Neal.[191] He originally enlisted in the army in December 1937.[192] He served in the Philippines and was honorably discharged. Following the attack on Pearl Harbor, he reenlisted. He trained at Fort Bragg, North Carolina, before going overseas in April 1942. He was killed in action in France. Ballard is buried at the American Cemetery & Memorial in Brittany, France. He is memorialized at Evergreen Cemetery in Lee, New York.

Earl F. Hawkridge

Birth: Around 1924, Montreal, Ontario, Canada[193]
Death: September 9, 1942
Burial: Lost at Sea; Memorialized on the East Coast Memorial in Manhattan, New York

Earl Hawkridge's family arrived in the United States when he was the age of two. Hawkridge grew up near New York City before moving to North Brookfield.[194] He joined the Coast Guard in March 1942. He was assigned to the USCGC *Muskeget* as part of the North Atlantic Weather Patrol. The ship is believed to have been torpedoed by German U-boat *U-755*. The ship was not reported as missing until September 13, when a replacement ship arrived. According to the U-boat report, the ship was struck by two torpedoes roughly 425 miles northeast of St. John's, Newfoundland, Canada. None of the sailors' remains were recovered.

Erford M. Johnson

Birth: May 10, 1921, Plymouth, New York[195]
Death: June 9, 1942, Philippines
Burial: Manila American Cemetery and Memorial, Philippines; Memorial at the Leonardsville Cemetery, Brookfield, New York

Erford Johnson attended schools in South Otselic and DeRuyter. He worked as a farm laborer prior to his enlistment in June 1941. Erford was one of five brothers (including Leon, Leo, Devillo and Earl) who served in the military during World War II. Johnson trained at Fort Slocum, New York, before being assigned to the 31st Infantry, Company A, in the Philippines. He fought in numerous battles and was captured after the fall of Bataan on May 7, 1942. He was one of more than seventy thousand soldiers forced to endure the "Bataan Death March." His family received a letter in June 1945 from Major General J.A. Ulio that explained how he died:

> *It is with profound regret that I confirm the recent telegram informing you of the death of your son, Erford, who was previously reported missing in action in the Philippine Islands from the date of the surrender of Corregidor, 7 May 1942.*
>
> *An official message has now been received that he died on 9 June 1942 in a prisoner of war camp in the Philippine Islands as a result of dysentery.*
>
> *I realize the great suspense you have endured during this unfortunately long period of time and now the finality to those hopes which you have cherished for his safety. Although little may be said or done at this time to alleviate your grief, if is my fervent hope that later the knowledge that he gave his life for his country may be of sustaining comfort to you.*

His brother Leo was captured around the same time and survived for three years in a Japanese prison before he was liberated and returned home. The Johnson-Rogers American Legion Post No. 1482 was named in part after Erford.[196]

Harold E. Loomis

Birth: February 24, 1920, Hubbardsville, New York[197]
Death: August 1, 1944, France
Burial: Normandy American Cemetery and Memorial, France; Memorial, Graham Cemetery, Hubbardsville, New York

Harold Loomis graduated from Brookfield Central School in June 1935.[198] Prior to the war, he worked as a gas attendant at an auto garage.[199] Loomis was inducted into the army in March 1942. He trained at Camp Livingston in Louisiana, Camp Gordon in Florida and Camp Pickett in Virginia. He went overseas to England in October 1943. He was killed in action in France and was posthumously awarded the Purple Heart.

Dighton Polan

Birth: December 10, 1917, Nortonville, Kansas
Death: December 4, 1945
Burial: Lost at Sea; Memorialized, Honolulu Courts of the Missing, Hawaii

Dighton Polan's father, Herbert Polan, was a minister, and the family moved a number of times during Dighton's childhood, including to Nebraska, Columbus (Chenango County, New York) and Brookfield, New York. He graduated from Brookfield Central School in 1936 and was the class valedictorian.[200] He enrolled at Salem College in West Virginia before transferring to Alfred University, graduating in 1939. He took a job teaching in Galway, New York, before enrolling in the navy in December 1940. He trained at Floyd Bennet Field in Long Island and in Jacksonville, Florida, where he was commissioned as an ensign in September 1941. He received specialized training at Banana River and Key West, Florida, as well as Norfolk, Virginia. In 1942, he was transferred to San Diego, California, for preparation to go to the Pacific Theater. While there, he married Edith Jane Wolf of Woodhaven, New York, on February 20, 1942. The married couple spent eight days together before he was sent overseas. On October 15, 1942, the plane he was flying was attacked and crashed at sea. He was listed as missing in action, lost at sea. He was on the same plane as Robert R. Sayers of Canastota. Polan was officially declared dead on December 4, 1945. He was posthumously awarded the Purple Heart.

Douglas Irving Rice

Birth: November 27, 1921, Ilion, New York[201]
Death: July 21, 1945, Pacific Theater
Burial: Brookfield Rural Cemetery, New York

After graduating from Ilion High School in 1942, Douglas Rice enlisted in the navy.[202] He trained in Newport, Rhode Island, and at the Wentworth Institute in Massachusetts. He was assigned to the USS *Alcar* in October 1942. He married Mary Steinburg of Rockport, Massachusetts, in 1944.[203] He took part in the invasions of Africa, Sicily and Italy before being assigned to the Pacific Theater.[204] He achieved the rank of machinist's mate first class. Rice was wounded on a ship and transferred to a hospital, where he died. His remains were returned in 1949. Douglas's brother Victor was killed the year before while serving in the navy.

Victor Lee Rice

Birth: December 18, 1907, Ilion, New York[205]
Death: July 1, 1943, New Georgia
Burial: Remains Not Recovered; Memorial, Brookfield Rural Cemetery, New York

Victor Rice graduated from Ilion High School in 1937 and joined the navy in May 1940. He trained in Newport, Rhode Island; Norfolk, Virginia; and

San Francisco, California.[206] In the fall of 1941, he was assigned to the USS *Whitney*, which he was on in Pearl Harbor, Hawaii, when the Japanese army attacked on December 7, 1941. He survived the attack and was transferred to the USS *McCawley*. The ship was attacked on June 30, 1943, near New Georgia. A letter to the family from Captain Robert H. Rodgers noted:

> *On June 30th while engaged in offensive action against a Japanese held island in the Solomon area the USS McCawley was sunk by an enemy torpedo plane…*
>
> *During this action your son was serving at his general quarter's station in the main engine room. The first of the three torpedoes which destroyed the McCawley hit her outside the middle section of the engine room and as a result 15 men on duty there are missing. The engine room was completely isolated they were never seen again and were reported as missing in action rather than killed. Victor was one of these men and as Captain of the McCawley it is my sad responsibility to report this to you and the circumstances attending it. I am sure there was no suffering involved.*
>
> *May the knowledge that your son was at a hero's station, serving nobly his country in its struggle for life and freedom, bring some consolation to the dark and lonely moments that are now yours because of this great loss.*
>
> *I know Victor was proud as we all are, of this important part which the McCawley has played in the South Pacific to date, and it has been my great privilege to have been the ship's captain.*

Victor's brother Douglas was killed in action in 1945.

Royce H. Rogers

Birth: March 9, 1920, Brookfield, New York[207]
Death: March 15, 1945, Germany
Burial: Brookfield Rural Cemetery, New York

Royce Rogers graduated from Brookfield Central School in 1938 and Morrisville State School 1940. He married Mary Jane Brown on June 21, 1941. Prior to his time in the service, he operated a garage in Brookfield. He joined the Quartermaster Corps in March 1943, training at Camp Upton in North Carolina. He was transferred to the U.S. Army Air Corps and continued his training in California and Oregon. Rogers's final training was for infantry in Paris, Texas, before being sent overseas in February 1945 as an infantry replacement. He was killed in action in Germany. The American Legion Post No. 1492 in Leonardsville, New York, was named the Johnson-Rogers Post in part for Royce.

HUGH SHERIDAN STONE JR.

Birth: September 29, 1923, New Milford, Pennsylvania[208]
Death: October 25, 1943, England
Burial: New Milford Cemetery, Pennsylvania

Hugh Stone attended schools in Brookfield and Norwich. Prior to joining the army, he worked at the Norwich Pharmacal Company. He enlisted in December 1942 and trained at Fort Niagara in New York.[209] He then trained as an infantryman in Company E, 2nd Battalion, 156th Infantry, at Sault St. Marie until he went overseas in August [210] Stone died after being shot in action. His remains were returned home in January 1949.

ELMER P. WHEELER

Birth: November 23, 1919, West Winfield, New York[211]
Death: June 10, 1944, France
Burial: Sunset Cemetery, Clinton, New York

Elmer Wheeler was the salutatorian of the Bridgewater Central School, class of 1938. Following his graduation, he worked for Grove W. Hinman in Madison, New York. He entered the army in February 1942.[212] He received training at Fort Dix in New Jersey, Camp Gordon in Florida and Fort Jackson in South Carolina. He went overseas in January 1944. He was wounded in action in France during the D-Day invasion and died of those wounds four days later. Wheeler was posthumously awarded the Purple Heart. His remains were returned home in 1948.[213]

John D. Williams

Birth: June 27, 1914, Plainfield, New York[214]
Death: December 25, 1944, Luxembourg
Burial: Luxembourg American Cemetery, Luxembourg

John attended school at DeLancey's Corners. He married Elinor Brown on June 27, 1935, and they had two daughters, Carolyn and Patricia. Williams joined the army in April 1944 and trained at Camp Croft in South Carolina and Fort George Meade in Maryland before going overseas in October 1944.[215] He attained the rank of staff sergeant. He was reported missing in action in January 1945. Two months later, a formal notice arrived that he was killed in action in Luxembourg.

CAZENOVIA

Donald William Aldrich

Birth: January 22, 1927, Watertown, New York[216]
Death: February 19, 1945, Iwo Jima
Burial: Indian Mound Cemetery, Moravia, New York

Following the death of his father, Donald Aldrich's family moved to Cazenovia, where he attended school before moving to Cayuga County. He joined the Marine Corps in 1943. Aldrich took part in the invasion of the Marianas. He was killed in action at the Battle of Iwo Jima.[217] His brother received a letter from Lieutenant General Alexander Vandegrift, the Marine Corps commanding officer, that stated:

> *Please accept our deepest sympathy in your great loss. It is my earnest hope that you will find some measure of consolation in knowing that your brother maintained a splendid record in the Corps and gave his life in the performance of his duty against the enemies of this country.*

John C. Baitsholts

Birth: April 16, 1923, Groton, New York[218]
Death: February 20, 1944, Germany
Burial: Ardennes American Cemetery and Memorial, Belgium

John Baitsholts graduated from New Woodstock High School in 1941 and enlisted in the U.S. Army Air Corps in July 1941. He attended basic training at Langley Field, Virginia, before being sent to Newfoundland in November 1941. He returned to Langley as a bomber engineer before attending additional pilot training in Texas and Louisiana. He flew a B-17 overseas to England in November 1943. He was reported missing after a bombing raid over Germany in February 1944. His last contact was thirty miles west of Leipzig, Germany.

Louis W. Buckingham

Birth: May 1, 1917, New Woodstock, New York[219]
Death: December 9, 1944, France
Burial: New Woodstock Cemetery, New York

Louis Buckingham graduated from New Woodstock High School in 1935.[220] Following graduation, Buckingham worked at his father's car dealership and repair shop and was a volunteer firefighter. He joined the army in October 1942 and was assigned to a tank regiment; he was trained as a gunner. Buckingham was killed during the Battle of the Bulge in France.[221] His company was charged with helping stop the enemy from breaking through. His remains were returned to the United States in June 1949.

Arthur L. Bush

Birth: May 27, 1913, Kent, England[222]
Death: January 18, 1945, Belgium
Burial: New Woodstock Cemetery, New York

Arthur Bush came to the United States at a young age and lived in Ridgefield, Connecticut. Following his graduation from school, Bush and his family moved to New Woodstock, New York. He attended Morrisville Agricultural College and Technical Institute. He married Ruth Wilcox of DeRuyter on December 10, 1937. They had a daughter, Janet. He worked as a farmer and later owned a wholesale retail Atlantic Gas and Oil service, which his wife operated while he was overseas. Bush joined the army in April 1944. He trained at Fort Dix in New Jersey, Camp Croft in South

Carolina, Fort George Meade in Maryland and Camp Shanks in New York. He went to Europe in September 1944. He was reported missing in action in February 1945. In March, he was reported as killed in action. His remains were returned to the United States in 1948.

Eugene K. Cook

Birth: February 7, 1915, New York[223]
Death: October 17, 1944, Italy
Burial: Evergreen Cemetery, Cazenovia, New York

Eugene Cook graduated from Cazenovia Central School in 1934 and enrolled at Morrisville Agricultural and Technical Institute in 1936.[224] Following his graduation, he moved to Erie County and worked for the Dairymen's League as a tester until 1938, when he moved to Clearwater, Florida, where he worked at the Clearwater Beach Hotel. He married Lilly McKenzie around 1940, and they had a daughter. He joined the army in January 1944 and took his basic training at Camp Blanding, Florida. He took secondary training at Fort George Meade, Maryland, before being sent to Italy in July 1944. He died from wounds received in action in Italy.

Donald M. Davis

Birth: February 3, 1920, Cazenovia, New York[225]
Death: July 5, 1943, Florida
Burial: St. Agnes Cemetery, Cazenovia, New York

Donald Davis graduated from Cazenovia Central School in 1941 and then attended the Mechanics Institute in Rochester.[226] He enlisted in the U.S. Army Air Corps in January 1942. He was commissioned an officer after completing cadet navigation training in Coral Gables in January 1943. He continued training in Carlsbad, New Mexico, before he was stationed with the 596th Squadron at MacDill Field in Tampa, Florida.[227] While in Florida, Davis was diagnosed with appendicitis; he was sent to Orlando and underwent an operation on June 9, 1943. He died from complications from the surgery.

William G. Haines Jr.

Birth: May 1, 1924, Erieville, New York[228]
Death: August 13, 1944, France
Burial: Cambridge American Cemetery and Memorial, England.

William Haines's father, William G. Haines Sr., was a veteran of World War I. Junior lived in Cazenovia until his family moved to Syracuse after completing his junior year of high school. He graduated from Nottingham High School in 1942, enrolled at Syracuse University and joined the Army Air Force Reserve in September 1942.[229] He was called to active duty after completing his first year at Syracuse. Haines trained as a navigator in multiple places, including Cleveland, Ohio, and at Ellington Field in Texas. He was commissioned a second lieutenant in April 1944. He was assigned to Alexandria Air Field in Louisiana before being sent overseas in June 1944. Many of Haines's letters were published in the *Cazenovia Republican*. In a letter published in June 1944, he talked about his training:

> *I'm in B-17 Phase training now and it has certainly come up to all the stories I heard about keeping one busy. I've had just about 15 hours' sleep in the last 86—three of which I got at 17,000 feet on the bombing range!! We fly every day, mostly at altitude. This last session was especially rough as we had three straight morning missions, briefing at 0530 which means getting up at 0430—what with Ground School 'till 6:00 PM—by the time we've eaten and cleaned up it's 9:30. When you write a letter, or two—well you can see how every possible it is to find yourself with only 5 hours "sack time."*
>
> *I was quite disappointed not to get a leave when I graduated. About one-half of my class didn't and I was in—as you might know—the unlucky half. For a while we thought we might get one here, but I guess it's impossible. I had a reservation to New York and I had planned to spend three or four days in Syracuse and Cazenovia. At this point though, I'm afraid I'm going to miss you. Out of the 57 Navigators I came here with, not one of us has had a leave or furlough, and now, I believe, we are going to go overseas with not even getting home once—it's not the most pleasant thing to think about and, needless to say, we are all just a little bit bitter. I had thought that everyone did get home before they left the country, but as a major told us, "Gentlemen, you are in the army." And I guess that sums the whole thing up rather neatly!*

> *I have received several letters from a good many of my old friends in Cazenovia since I graduated and I have been too busy to answer them. Please, all of you, don't think I don't appreciate your writing. I shall surely try to answer everyone of them when I can. But I'm hoping you'll understand that if I am very late doing it it's not my fault!!*
>
> *The crew I am with are a great bunch of boys. The pilot and co-pilot are both married, but the bombardier is single so he and I get along fine. They are all from California. I'm afraid I was a bit of a disappointment coming from New York, but as I told them, the army gives at least one New Yorker to every crew for good luck….!!!*[230]

Haines flew approximately thirty-five missions overseas.[231] He was killed in action in France. He was posthumously awarded the Purple Heart.

Bruce E. Jenkins (Jankins)

Birth: August 12, 1922, Poland, New York[232]
Death: January 11, 1945, Island of Luzon
Burial: Newport Cemetery, New York

Bruce Jenkins attended school in Perryville. Jenkins joined the army in Hartford, Connecticut, in March 1941.[233] In letters home, he talks about his experiences in the Pacific Theater.[234] He visited New Zealand, New Caledonia, Guadalcanal, Russell Island, New Georgia and Banga. He took part in combat on New Georgia and Banga. He died from wounds he received on the Island of Luzon. His remains were returned in 1948.

Howard R. Lieurance

Birth: July 11, 1916, Canejous, Colorado[235]
Death: October 27, 1943, Italy
Burial: Sicily-Rome Cemetery and Memorial, Italy

Howard Lieurance's family moved to DeRuyter while he was still a toddler. He graduated from Cazenovia Central School in 1936.[236] Following graduation, he attended a prep school in Tarrytown, New York. He spent three summers attending the Civilians Army Training Camps at Fort Niagara (two years) and Plattsburgh. Prior to the war, he worked at Continental Can Company and the Cazenovia Electric Company. Lieureance enlisted in April 1941 and attended Officers Training School at Fort Benning, Georgia. He was commissioned a lieutenant upon graduation. He married Adeline Berrena of Harrisburg, Pennsylvania, on December 17, 1942.[237] Following their marriage, he was assigned to Camp McCoy in Wisconsin. Lieurance was killed in action in Italy. He was posthumously awarded the Purple Heart and the Distinguished Service Cross.[238] The citation for the Distinguished Service Cross reads:

> *While preparing to lead his platoon in an attack on a strongly entrenched enemy position, Second Lieutenant Lieurance was mortally wounded by hostile machine gun fire. Although suffering intense pain, he summoned his squad leaders to report to him. Under intense machine gun fire from positions only 150 yards away and under constant enemy artillery and mortar shelling, he issued his detailed plan of attack. Second Lieutenant Lieurance lapsed into unconsciousness despite prompt first aid treatment, but as a result of his calm and courageous self-control in completing preparations for the attack, his men were inspired to carry out a successful operation. His leadership, bravery, and devotion to duty reflect the highest traditions of the Army of the United States.*[239]

Thomas McNulty

Birth: November 26, 1907, Donegal, Ireland[240]
Death: May 9, 1945, Germany[241]
Burial: Jefferson Barracks National Cemetery, Lemay, Missouri

Thomas McNulty's family came to Cazenovia around 1920, and he worked as a baker following school. He attended the American Institute of Baking in Chicago and returned to work at Cazenovia Bakery. He moved to Miami, Florida, at some point and later to Minneapolis, Minnesota.[242] He was working as a chemist at the T.C. Milk Producers Association in Minnesota when he joined the U.S. Army Air Corps around 1941. He obtained the rank of technical sergeant.[243] He was killed in action while serving as a turret gunner on a bombing mission. He was posthumously awarded the Purple Heart.

EDWARD O. MILLER

Birth: May 19, 1924, Manlius, New York[244]
Death: April 16, 1945, Italy
Burial: Manlius Village Cemetery, Manlius, New York

Edward Miller graduated from Cazenovia Central School in 1943 and entered the army medical corps in September 1943.[245] Miller trained at Camp Barkley in Texas and Camp Reynolds in Pennsylvania.[246] He was killed in action in Italy.[247] He was posthumously awarded the Purple Heart, which was given to his mother, Alice Miller.[248] Edward's remains were returned in 1948.

ALBERT J. POTTER JR.

Birth: March 17, 1919, Syracuse, New York[249]
Death: January 8, 1945, Belgium
Burial: Luxembourg American Cemetery and Memorial, Luxembourg

Albert Potter graduated from Vocational High School and was also a student at Cazenovia Seminary. Following graduation, he enrolled in Syracuse University. Potter joined the army in July 1941. He trained in the States and was sent overseas in September 1944.[250] He married Arbutus A. Morgan of Cazenovia in Fort Benning, Georgia, on July 24, 1943.[251] Potter was assigned to an armored field artillery unit in the 3rd Army. He was killed in action in Belgium during the Battle of the Bulge. He was posthumously awarded the Purple Heart.[252]

MALCOLM S. TAYLOR

Birth: March 7, 1919, New Woodstock, New York[253]
Death: May 5, 1943, Iceland
Burial: New Woodstock Cemetery, New York

Malcolm Taylor graduated from New Woodstock High School in 1936 and worked as a farm laborer following his graduation.[254] He entered the U.S. Army Air Corps in March 1941 and trained at the Aberdeen Proving

Grounds in Maryland, March Field and Muroc, California. He obtained the rank of staff sergeant in July 1942. In February 1943, Taylor was assigned to Iceland. He was the first resident of Cazenovia killed during the war when he died during an accident. His remains were returned home in 1947.

Harvey Eric Trammell Jr.

Birth: January 9, 1926, Washington, D.C.[255]
Death: December 28, 1944, France
Burial: St. Agnes Cemetery, Syracuse, New York

Harvey Trammell Jr.'s father died in Rio de Janeiro, Brazil, while serving in the U.S. Diplomatic Corps in 1942. Trammell Jr. attended Manlius Military Academy and after graduation enrolled in Brown University, majoring in engineering. He left the school in December 1943 and enrolled in the Army Specialized Training Program at Cornell University. From there, he attended basic training at Camp Wheeler in Georgia and further training at Fort Bragg in North Carolina. He was sent overseas in October 1944. Trammell was severely wounded in action in France on December 20, 1944, and he died from those wounds eight days later.

Fred L. Waffner

Birth: June 26, 1919, Fabius, New York[256]
Death: March 7, 1945, Iwo Jima
Burial: New Woodstock Cemetery, New York

Fred Waffner attended schools in Fabius and Cazenovia and worked as a machine setter at the Easy Washer Corporation in Syracuse, New York, prior to the war. He married Esther Ione Cossitt on June 21, 1938, in New Woodstock, New York.[257] They had two sons, Bernard and Robert, and a daughter, Nancy.[258] Waffner joined the U.S. Marine Corps in June 1944. He trained at Parris Island, South Carolina, and Camp Lejeune, North Carolina. He was sent to the Pacific Theater in November 1944. He died from wounds he suffered in action during the Battle of Iwo Jima. His remains were returned in 1948.

Bernard J. Works

Birth: January 18, 1920, Syracuse, New York[259]
Death: July 10, 1944, France
Burial: St. Mary's Cemetery, DeWitt, New York

Bernard Works graduated from Cathedral Academy in Syracuse and worked at the Onondaga Pottery Company prior to enlisting.[260] He married Connie Pullman in Cazenovia on September 19, 1942. The couple had a son, Stephen Robert, who was born in 1943, and a daughter, Judith Ann, who was born in December 1944 after Bernard died.[261] Works joined the Army Combat Engineers in March 1943. He attended basic training at Camp White in Oregon and further training at Fort Lewis in Washington, Fort Pierce in Florida and Camp Pickett in Virginia. Works was sent overseas in April 1944. He was killed in action in France.

DeRuyter

James H. Hinds

Birth: January 25, 1920, DeRuyter, New York[262]
Death: March 13, 1945, Germany
Burial: Hillcrest Cemetery, DeRuyter, New York

James Hinds graduated from DeRuyter Central School in 1937. He married Martha Warren in DeRuyter on June 23, 1940. They had one daughter, Claudia Martha Hinds. Prior to entering the service, Hinds worked at the Solvay Process Company in Solvay, New York. He entered the service in November 1943 and received his basic training at Camp Lee in Virginia. He took further training at Camp Reynolds in Pennsylvania. He was sent overseas to Europe in July 1944. He was killed in action in Germany. In a letter to his wife, Captain William R. Smith wrote of what happened:

> *May I, on behalf of the officers and men of Company "G" extend to you our condolences on the passing of your husband, Private James H. Hinds, 42026248, who was killed in action against the enemy on the 13th of March, 1945 in the vicinity of Linz, Germany.*
>
> *I am sure that it will be a comfort to you to know that James was laid to rest at an American cemetery in eastern Belgium with full military honors. A Protestant Chaplain performed the final rites.*

James was guarding an advance in the Remagen Bridgehead and was killed as a result of Enemy aerial bombing. He was identified by two of his comrades.

During the brief period that James was in this organization, he was always a most valued member. The thorough and cheerful manner in which he performed his various duties won him a host of friends among his fellow soldiers and the respect and admiration of his officers. His performance of duty was in the highest traditions of the American soldier. He will be greatly missed by all members of this organization who join me in extending to you our most sincere sympathy for your great loss.[263]

Hinds's remains were returned home in 1947.

Robert Powers

Birth: November 30, 1921, Lapwai, Idaho
Death: April 2, 1943, North Africa
Burial: Hillcrest Cemetery, DeRuyter, New York

Robert Powers's family moved to South Otselic in 1927 and later moved to DeRuyter. He graduated from DeRuyter Central School in 1938. He enrolled at Cornell University and was a junior there when he enlisted in the U.S. Army Air Corps in November 1941. He was an aviation cadet at Maxwell Field in Alabama and Craig Field in Selma, Alabama, before receiving his commission in November 1942. Following his commission, he was stationed at Langley Field in Virginia until he was sent overseas to North Africa. He seemed nostalgic while talking about his hope for the future in his last letter home:

Sometimes I remember the past and think I would like to be back there where I had so few troubles and responsibilities. It would be nice—but I really wouldn't want to go back. The uncertainty of the future calls, and I must go on and on, filled with the desire to see what the future holds for us who fight and hope.

Powers was killed in action in North Africa. His remains were returned in 1948.[264]

Harlow M. Truman

Birth: July 7, 1917, New Woodstock, New York[265]
Death: August 7, 1944, France
Burial: Normandy American Cemetery, France

Harlow Truman graduated from DeRuyter Central School and attended Alfred University. Prior to entering the war, he was employed by Cossitt Brothers of Hamilton.[266] Truman enlisted in the U.S. Army Air Corps in July 1942. He trained at Nashville, Tennessee; Maxwell Field in Alabama; and Shaw Field in South Carolina. He was commissioned a second lieutenant in November 1943 and was assigned to Barksdale Field, Louisiana. Truman was sent overseas in March 1944. He was the copilot on a B-26 Marauder that crashed in France. He was originally listed as missing in action, but in May 1945, he was declared killed in action. Following his death, his family received his Air Medal Award with four Oak Leaf Clusters for "meritorious achievement over enemy occupied territory."

EATON

Charles W. Clark

Birth: August 30, 1922, Eaton, New York[267]
Death: September 1, 1944, Germany[268]
Burial: Ardennes American Cemetery and Memorial, Belgium

Charles Clark grew up in New York and Wisconsin. Charles graduated from Belmont High School in Allegany County and then enrolled at the Alfred Agricultural and Technical School. Following graduation, he worked for the Rochester Gas & Electric Company in Belmont. His father, Neil, took a position teaching auto mechanics at the Morrisville Agricultural & Technical Institute at this time, and the remainder of Clark's family moved to Morrisville. Clark enlisted in the U.S. Army Air Corps in 1942 and trained as a B-17 pilot.[269] He was part of the first American flight over Berlin during the war and flew multiple flights over Berlin. For his actions, he received the Air Medal and an Oak Leaf Cluster. Clark's plane failed to return from a mission in March 1944. He was declared dead in October 1944, and his family received a letter from Major General J.A. Ulio:

> *Your son was reported missing in action on a mission to Brunswick, Germany on 23 March 1944. The War Department has now received an official report that your son was killed in action 23 March 1944 when his plane was attacked and destroyed by enemy fighter planes near Oldenberg, Germany.*
>
> *I know the sorrow this message has brought you and it is my hope that in time the knowledge of his heroic sacrifice in the service of his country may be of sustaining comfort to you.*[270]

Clark was posthumously awarded a Purple Heart.

Michael Denega

Birth: February 1, 1920, Auburn, New York[271]
Death: January 12, 1945, Southwest Pacific[272]
Burial: Manila American Cemetery and Memorial, Philippines

Michael Denega worked as a baker at the Rome State School prior to the war.[273] He grew up in Skaneateles and married Shirley Church of Hamilton on November 21, 1940.[274] They had a daughter, Sharon, around 1942. Denega joined the Army Corps of Engineers in June 1943.[275] He trained at Westover Field in Massachusetts and in Richmond, Virginia. He was sent overseas in February 1944. Denega was killed in action in the southwest Pacific.

Alan H. Mosher

Birth: May 18, 1925, Old Forge, New York[276]
Death: December 8, 1944, France
Burial: Pinecrest Cemetery, Lake Worth, Florida

Alan Mosher grew up in Old Forge, DeRuyter and Morrisville before his family moved to Florida following his junior year of high school. Mosher's father, Frank, was a World War I veteran and served as a corporal in the Engineers Battalion in World War II. His brother Bruce was in the U.S.

Merchant Marines. Alan enlisted in the army in September 1943.[277] He trained at Fort Benning in Georgia before being sent overseas. Mosher was killed in action in France.

Francis Sisbower

Birth: January 24, 1923, Eaton, New York[278]
Death: August 1, 1944, Belgium[279]
Burial: Epinal American Cemetery and Memorial, France

Francis Sisbower lived in Eaton before moving to Jacksonville, Florida, prior to 1935.[280] Prior to going overseas, Sisbower married Billie K. Sisk,[281] and they had a daughter, Joyce Dean Sisbower, in Gastonia, North Carolina, on August 22, 1942.[282] He enlisted in the army in Jacksonville, Florida, in October 1940.[283] He trained at Fort Bragg in North Carolina and Fort Dix in New Jersey. In May 1943, he was sent overseas and took part in the invasions of North Africa, Italy, France and Germany. Sisbower was killed in action during the Battle of the Bulge in Belgium. He was posthumously awarded the Purple Heart and the Combat Infantry Badge. Sisbower's father, also Francis, was awarded the Purple Heart after suffering significant injuries during World War I.

Edward R. Smith

Birth: September 8, 1923, San Francisco, California[284]
Death: May 21, 1944, Hawaii[285]
Burial: Remains Not Recovered; Memorialized at the Courts of the Missing, Honolulu, Hawaii

Edward Smith graduated from Morrisville High School before joining the Naval Reserve in November 1942. He trained in New York, California and Washington before going overseas in June 1943.[286] He achieved the rank of pharmacist mate third class. Smith was killed at sea because of an accidental explosion (possibly the West Loch Disaster at Pearl Harbor, Hawaii).

Howard A. Smith

Birth: April 27, 1912, West Eaton, New York[287]
Death: December 30, 1944, Leyte
Burial: West Eaton Cemetery, New York

Howard Smith graduated from Eaton High School and worked at bakeries in Earlville and Tully before going to work for the Brown Lipe Chapin plant in Syracuse.[288] He joined the army in June 1942, climbing to the rank of staff sergeant. He married Ann Uhl of Syracuse. He trained Fort Meade in Maryland and Camp Livingston in Louisiana. Smith went overseas in December 1943, initially to New Guinea and later to the island of Leyte.[289] On December 15, 1944, he was diagnosed with "tropical fever" (acute hepatitis) and died fifteen days later. Smith's remains were returned home in 1948.[290]

Ralph A. Snyder

Birth: December 22, 1907, West Danby, New York[291]
Death: February 11, 1945, Mississippi
Burial: Inlet Valley Cemetery, Ithaca, New York

Ralph Snyder graduated from Spencer High School. His family moved to Morrisville after his father accepted a position as principal of Morrisville High School, and his mother became a first-grade teacher. Snyder enrolled at Colgate University in 1925 and graduated in 1929. He attended Albany Law School for two years. Prior to enlisting, he worked for the Burgess Independent Oil Company of Utica and International Harvester Company of Glens Falls. He took a job as an outside salesman for the Murray Brothers of Honesdale, Pennsylvania, in 1938. He married Blanche B. Brenhofer in Milton, Pennsylvania, on September 5, 1943.[292] He enlisted in the U.S. Army Air Corps in December 1942. He qualified for special training and studied psychology in Pennsylvania before being stationed in Baltimore, Maryland, and Belvoir, Mississippi. He died of pneumonia in a hospital in Mississippi.

SYLVESTER N. WESTCOTT

Birth: September 10, 1923, Eaton, New York[293]
Death: December 31, 1944, Germany
Burial: Lorraine American Cemetery, France

Sylvester Westcott attended local schools but was forced to work prior to his graduation. He worked for Oneida Limited in the surgical department prior to joining the service. He married Luella Towsley in 1943, and they had a son. He joined the army in January 1943. He trained at Camp Upton in New York, Louisiana, Camp Hood in Texas and Camp Borvie in Oklahoma.[294] Westcott was assigned to the 824th Tank Destroyer Battalion. He went overseas in October 1944. Westcott was originally reported missing in action in January 1945, but he was later reported killed in action in Germany.

ALBERT R. WILT

Birth: July 19, 1921, Morrisville, New York[295]
Death: May 20, 1944, Austria[296]
Burial: Lorraine American Cemetery, Lorraine, France

Albert Wilt graduated from Morrisville-Eaton Central School in 1939.[297] Following graduation, he worked as a laborer and later at the Savage Arms Corporation in Utica. He joined the U.S. Army Air Corps in 1943 and trained at Selman Field in Louisiana, Davis-Monthan Field in Arizona, Will Rogers Field in Oklahoma, Langley Field in Virginia and in Topeka, Kansas. He trained as a navigator on the B-24 airplane. He was sent overseas to Africa and Italy. He was serving as a navigator on a B-17 "Flying Fortress" over Austria when he was declared missing in June 1944. He was declared dead in December 1944.[298]

FENNER

Edmund Joseph Burke

Birth: March 8, 1915, East Syracuse, New York[299]
Death: October 3, 1943, New Guinea[300]
Burial: Unknown

Edmund Burke graduated from Canastota High School in 1933.[301] He enrolled at Colgate and graduated with the class of 1939; he also played on the football team. In 1939, Burke moved to Utica and took a job with Savage Arms. He enlisted in the navy in September 1942. Burke was serving aboard the USS *Henley* in October when it was torpedoed off the coast of New Guinea.[302] He was listed as missing before being declared dead in November 1944. Burke's remains were never recovered.

Grant C. Schaff

Birth: May 1, 1923, Endicott, New York[303]
Death: July 28, 1943, North Sea[304]
Burial: Remains Not Found; Memorialized at Netherlands American Cemetery and Memorial, Netherlands

Grant Schaff grew up in Fenner and attended Cazenovia Schools, graduating from Cazenovia Central School in 1942.[305] Schaff enlisted in September

1942 into the U.S. Army Air Corps. He trained at the Aerial Gunnery School at Tyndall Field in Florida and Radio School in Salt Lake City, Utah. He was then stationed in Washington, Nebraska and Montana. He was declared missing after his plane did not return from a bombing raid over Germany on July 28, 1943. He was declared dead a year later.[306] According to letters the family received following the missing in action report, the plane went down over the North Sea, and only two men survived the crash. At the time of his death, he was engaged to Barbara Hughes of Cazenovia.

BERNARD C. SEITZ

Birth: September 23, 1918, Oneida, New York[307]
Death: June 4, 1942, Midway Island[308]
Burial: Remains Not Recovered; Court of the Missing, Honolulu Memorial

Bernard Seitz graduated from Oneida High School and worked in his father's bakery business prior to his induction in the U.S. Army Air Corps in July 1941.[309] He trained in Augusta, Georgia, and Tampa, Florida, as a gunner. On June 4, 1942, Seitz took part in the first torpedo attack ever carried out by the air force, according to the following notice. His plane did not return. He posthumously received the Purple Heart and Distinguished Service Cross for his actions:

> *Bernard C. Seitz, Corporal, 69th Bombardment Squadron (M), Army Air Forces, United States Army. For extraordinary heroism in action near Midway Island, 4 June 1942. Corporal Seitz as a gunner of a medium bombardment airplane displayed extraordinary heroism during a torpedo-bombing mission against the Japanese Navy. The success of the mission was dependent entirely upon the skill, courageousness and unfaltering devotion to duty of the crewmembers of the airplanes participating, who unhesitatingly entered into the attack at great personal risk to their lives in the face of concentrated gunfire of the Japanese Naval forces and fighter planes. During this, the first torpedo attack ever carried out by the Army Air Forces, the airplane on which Corporal Seitz was gunner was lost.*[310]

Seitz was declared dead one year later.

William Henry Seitz Jr.

Birth: October 4, 1921, New York[311]
Death: August 5, 1944, California[312]
Burial: St. Agatha's Cemetery, Canastota, New York

William Seitz Jr. graduated from Canastota High School and enrolled at the New York State College of Agriculture at Cornell University before enlisting in the U.S. Army Air Corps in December 1942. He was commissioned a second lieutenant in the 450th Army Air Force.[313] He trained at camps in Kansas, Texas, Florida and California. Seitz was killed during a training flight in Leach Lake, California.

GEORGETOWN

Frederick J. Sherman Jr.

Birth: September 7, 1925, Geneva, New York[314]
Death: October 13, 1944, France[315]
Burial: Lorraine American Cemetery and Memorial, France

Frederick Sherman attended grade school in Geneva and Cazenovia before graduating from high school in Cincinnatus. He moved to Georgetown in 1942. He joined the army in December 1943. He trained with the 101st Infantry at Camp Blanding in Florida before being sent overseas in September 1944. Sherman was killed in action in France. He was posthumously awarded the Purple Heart.

Wilfred L. Trass

Birth: April 8, 1919, New York[316]
Death: March 6, 1944, Louisiana[317]
Burial: Hillcrest Cemetery, DeRuyter, New York

Wilfred Trass graduated from Georgetown Central School in 1937. He enrolled and graduated from Oswego State Teacher's College, majoring in industrial arts. While attending school, he worked as a cadet teacher at Oneida High School in 1941. Following graduation, he worked at the Company of Master Craftsmen until he was drafted in July 1943. He entered the U.S. Army Air Corps and trained as a bomber pilot, earning a commission as a second lieutenant. He was killed when the plane he was training on crashed and exploded near Castor, Louisiana.

HAMILTON

Thomas B. Bates

Birth: January 29, 1921, Massachusetts[318]
Death: January 22, 1944, Italy
Burial: Sicily-Rome American Cemetery & Memorial, Italy

Thomas Bates graduated from Thayer Academy in June 1939 and enrolled at Colgate University. While at Colgate, he was on the ski team and a ski jumper. He was working for the Quincy Mutual Fire Insurance Company prior to enlisting. He enlisted in the ski troops of the army in April 1942. He trained at Camp Devens in Massachusetts and Camp Roberts in California before entering Officers' Candidate School at Fort Benning in Georgia. He was commissioned a second lieutenant in January 1943. He was promoted to first lieutenant while serving as a personnel officer at Camp Hale in Colorado. Bates then volunteered to be a replacement soldier, and in October 1943, he was sent to North Africa, where he was assigned to the Fourth Ranger Battalion and sent to the Italian front. Bates was killed in action on January 22, 1944, by a sniper during the invasion of Anzio, Italy.[319] According to a letter from Corporal Bob Carroll to his family:

> *It was on the morning of Jan. 22 that I heard that the lieutenant was killed. It was the morning of the invasion of Anzio if you remember. I came ashore as the radio operator for our headquarters. If I remember correctly it was about 4 am that I got a message from one of our companies*

that a sniper had shot and wounded one of their officers and for us to send the doc up. By the time, the doc and his medics arrived to the spot the officer had died.

It was some time later that I went to see the Doc for something for my stomach, for I was feeling pretty rotten since the morning. It was then I asked the Doc who it was that was killed in the morning. He told me that it was a new officer named Lt. Thomas Bates.

That's all I remember, except that a couple of his boys got the sniper. The Doc told me that the bullet that killed him was one that hit him high in the chest, bursting a blood vessel.

Barclay Boyd Beeby

Birth: November 21, 1914, Alton, Illinois[320]
Death: December 30, 1944, Puerto Rico[321]
Burial: Arlington National Cemetery, Virginia

Barclay Beeby grew up in Alton, Illinois. He attended Alton High School and later Phillips Exeter Academy in New Hampshire. After graduating high school, he attended Colgate University. He was an All-Eastern end on the football team in 1937. After graduating from Colgate, Beeby returned home and worked as the sales manager for his parents' company, the Alton Baking and Ice Cream Company. He married Bernadette Coles in Festus, Missouri, on July 24, 1940.[322] Beeby was called to active duty in the U.S. Army Air Corps in April 1942. Following his training as a pilot of a B-17 Bomber, he was commissioned a lieutenant in January 1943 in Arizona. He continued training before going to England in June 1943. While overseas, Beeby flew twenty-five combat missions, including one on December 31, 1943, in which he was injured:

> [H]*is plane was forced out of formation after the propeller of one engine blew off. The propeller went through the side of the plane and wounded the bombardier. Rapidly losing altitude the ship became vulnerable prey for German fighters. Lieutenant Beeby found an empty field in France, ordered the bombs dropped and started back to England. Fire from a German fighter, which the Alton Flier's crew finally shot down, wounded the top turret gunner and Lieutenant Beeby but the plane with only one of the four motors going, reached England. After that Lieut. Beeby was*

> *hospitalized for a short time but he soon was back again at the controls of his ship flying over Germany.*[323]

During his time overseas, Beeby was awarded a Silver Star, the Distinguished Flying Cross, the Air Medal with three Oak Leaf Clusters and the Purple Heart. The citation on his Silver Start states that he was

> [S]*erving as Pilot of a B-17 Heavy Bomber on a bombing mission over enemy occupied Europe, 31 December 1943. When one engine of his aircraft became disabled prior to reaching the target, Lieutenant Beeby endeavored to maintain his position in the formation but soon found this to be impossible. Shortly afterwards, the propeller on the disabled engine sheared off its shaft and tore through the nose compartment causing serious damage and injuring the bombardier. Following this, enemy fighters attacked and as a result the ball turret guns were knocked out, three members of the crew wounded by exploding cannon shells, the oxygen system knocked out and a fire started in the cockpit. After extinguishing the fire, Lieutenant Beeby dove his plane to a low altitude and skillfully maneuvered his aircraft back to base.*[324]

Beeby returned home in March 1944 and was assigned to B-29 training for an extended period in Texas, New Mexico and Nebraska. In December 1944, he was sent to Puerto Rico to serve as an aviation instructor. He was killed when the plane he was training in crashed in Puerto Rico. Following his death, his parents set up a memorial fund in Beeby's name to benefit the Alton Memorial Hospital.[325] In 1981, a new wing of the hospital opened bearing his name.[326]

Donald Reed Brooks

Birth: May 2, 1912, Gardner, Massachusetts[327]
Death: September 23, 1944, Italy
Burial: Crystal Lake Cemetery, Gardner, Massachusetts

Donald Brooks attended Gardner High School and then enrolled at Colgate University.[328] Following his time at Colgate, he attended George Washington University and the Diplomatic and Consular Service Institute at Washington, D.C. He was working at the Simplex Time Recorder Company in D.C. He enlisted in the army in October 1942. He earned the rank of sergeant in the infantry and was sent to Italy. Brooks was seriously wounded on September 20, 1944. He died from those wounds three days later and was posthumously awarded multiple medals, including the Purple Heart and the Silver Star. He received the Silver Star for his actions on September 20, 1944:

> [G]*iven the task of covering his company's withdrawal from an exposed position in the face of intensive enemy machine gun fire, Sergeant Brooks, although he drew intense counter fire, tenaciously poured a heavy volume of fire at the enemy until he received a serious head wound. His courage and determination enabled the unit to withdraw without further casualties.*

William E. Burckhalter

Birth: September 9, 1921, Alameda, California[329]
Death: June 11, 1944, New Guinea
Burial: Lost at Sea; Memorialized at the Tablet of the Missing, Hawaii

William Burckhalter attended Hastings High School and enrolled at Colgate University. While at Colgate, he took ground courses in aviation. He enrolled in the navy in July 1942 and trained as a pilot. He trained in Florida, Connecticut and Virginia. He was sent to the Pacific Theater and took part in a number of actions. During the spring of 1944, he was credited with shooting down three Japanese Sallys during a single mission on April 21, 1944.[330] Burckhalter was awarded the Silver Star for the operations. The citation reads:

> [F]*or conspicuous gallantry and intrepidity in action as a fighter pilot in Fighting Squadron Sixteen during operations against Japanese-held bases at Hollandia, New Guinea, on 21 April 1944. After successfully engaging in an offensive strike against enemy airfields, he sighted a formation of three enemy twin-engine bombers, and after calling unsuccessfully for assistance proceeded to attack single-handed, the three planes. He successively attacked these planes, and by his courageous and aggressive actions and unusual skill, succeeded in the certain destruction of all three bombers, alone and unaided. By his actions, he indicated a complete disregard for his own personal safety which was in keeping with the highest traditions of the United States Navel Service.*

On June 11, 1944, Burckhalter once again went beyond the call of duty and was killed during a mission. In a letter to his mother, Commander Paul D. Buie explained what happened:

> *On the morning of June 11 (your time) "Burkey" participated in an attack against an enemy-held island and his plane was hit by their intense anti-aircraft fire. He attempted to land his crippled plane in the water off shore and was successful in doing so. His teammates circled the plane, but although the landing was good he was unable to disengage himself from the plane and we believe went down with it. Our aircraft circled the spot for twenty or thirty minutes but found no evidence to give us hope that he survived. In addition our ships crisscrossed the area for days without finding any further trace of him.*[331]

Along with his Silver Star, Burckhalter was also awarded the Air Medal and Distinguished Flying Cross.

Charles Duell

Birth: January 27, 1921, Hamilton, New York[332]
Death: December 3, 1943, Italy
Burial: Woodlawn Cemetery, Hamilton, New York

Charles Duell attended Brookfield High School before graduating from Hamilton High School. Following graduation, he enrolled and attended the Oswego Normal School. He enlisted with his brother Frederick in November 1940. Duell trained at Camp Dix in New Jersey, Camp Claiborne in Louisiana and then Fort Lewis in Washington. Following training, he was assigned to Officers' Candidate School. After graduating, he had two assignments before he went overseas in August 1943 as a member of the 142nd Infantry. Duell was killed in action in Italy. Duell's mother received a letter from Lieutenant W.F. Langman concerning his death:[333]

> *Charles' death occurred December 3rd, about 8 o'clock in the morning. I Company was attacking a hill. Charles' platoon was leading the assault*

platoon of the company. His platoon did a fine job and the attack was a success, due mainly to the work of Lieutenant Duell and his men. We recommended Charles for the award of the Silver Star and I believe it went through. The Silver Star is awarded for gallantry in action. I led the company to the line of departure, with Charles right behind me. When we reached the L.D. Charles was to take over, Charles stuck out his head and said "Good luck, Bill." That was typical of him. Another thing, Mrs. Duell, he did not suffer a bit. His death was instantaneous. He was leading his platoon.

For his actions that day, Duell was posthumously awarded the Silver Star:[334]

As his platoon attacked the left edge of the hill, Lieutenant Duell observed an enemy sniper preparing to throw a hand grenade from his dugout. Without hesitation and with utter disregard for his personal safety, he personally attacked the sniper but was struck by the grenade and fatally wounded. His self-sacrifice enabled his men to continue the advance. His gallant action reflects great credit upon himself and the Armed Forces of the United States.

Duell's remains were returned home in February 1949.

Richard Ives East

Birth: January 16, 1920, Detroit, Michigan[335]
Death: April 4, 1943, Tunisia[336]
Burial: North Africa American Cemetery & Memorial, Tunisia; Memorial, Birch Lake Cemetery Calvin Township, Michigan

Richard East grew up in New Jersey and enrolled at Colgate University, where he wrestled and played one year of football.[337] He left school during his senior year to enlist in the U.S. Army Air Corps in December 1941.[338] East trained to fly the RAF Spitfire as well as the P-40, and he was commissioned a second lieutenant. He earned his wings in September 1942. During training, East and his friend Captain Harold A. Taff each spent $1.25 and together bought a Springer Spaniel named Duckworth.[339] They brought the dog with them to the North African campaign. He wrote to his parents:

Duckworth "sweated it out" on the ground during battle missions and romped joyously on each safe return.

East was killed in action when his plane crashed at sea in April 1943. After his parents received notice of their son's death, they requested that Duckworth be returned home to them. The letter rose through the ranks and eventually made it to the desk of Dwight D. Eisenhower. Eisenhower contacted Lieutenant General Carl A. Spaatz, Allied air commander of the Northwest African Air Force, who then dispatched a member of his staff as well as a member of the Red Cross to find the dog. Eisenhower explained in a letter to the family:

> *When I received your letter asking for the return of the dog owned by your son I was deeply touched. I immediately directed that every effort be made to comply with your request. Today I received from General Spaatz a report in which appears the following statement:*
>
> *It is learned that the dog Duckworth belonged jointly to Lt. East and his best friend Harold Taff. Lt. East was killed in action April 4. His plane and grave were located after our forces moved into the Tunis area. The loss of his best friend deeply affected Taff. The commanding officer of the fighting group brought Taff with the dog to the airplane. Taff was heartbroken at the thought of losing his dog and wanted to spend every possible minute with him until the plane took off. He placed him in the plane and carefully tied him. He left the plane just before the takeoff. Col. West had been waiting in his car to take Taff back to his quarters but Taff was seen to thank him and walk away from the car to an adjoining field.*
>
> *Under the circumstances and in particular in view of the statement that the dog was jointly owned by your son and his best friend and especially as Taff has shown strong affection for the dog I believe you will agree with me it would be unwise to return the dog to you as requested.*
>
> *The friendship of a dog is precious. It becomes even more so when one is so far removed from home as we are in Africa. I have a Scottie. In him I find consolation and diversion. For me he is the "one" person to whom I can talk without the conversation turning back to the war. Duckworth is performing a patriotic service. I respect the quality of warm friendship shown by Taff and the dog. I am confident you and Mrs. East will view the situation similarly despite your natural and understandable desire to have with you this close companion of your gallant son who died for his country on the field of battle.*[340]

Eventually, Duckworth made it back to the East family during the fall of 1944. His family established the Richard Ives East Student Loan Fund as a memorial to him at Colgate University in 1945.[341]

Robert S. Gregory

Birth: October 23, 1916, Ogdensburg, New York[342]
Death: January 17, 1945, France
Burial: Vestal Hills Cemetery, Vestal, New York

Robert Gregory moved with his family at a young age to Broome County and attended East Junior High School before graduating from Binghamton High School in 1933. Following graduation, he enrolled at Colgate University, graduating in 1937. Gregory then enrolled in Harvard Law School, graduating in 1940 and joining the New York State Bar Association in 1941. In May 1941, he entered the army and graduated from Officers' Candidate School in 1942, earning a commission as a second lieutenant. He continued training at Fort Campbell in Kentucky and Camp Barkley in Texas before going to Europe in September 1944. He was promoted to captain and served in an armored division. He was killed in action at the Rhine River near Strasbourg.[343] Following his death, he was awarded a Bronze Star.[344] The citation reads:

> *He led his company in attack on Ollendorf and Herrlisheim France, displaying coolness and good judgment under very heavy fire of artillery, mortar, rifle and anti-tank guns.*
>
> *After his tank was destroyed by fire, he continued to direct the operations of his company from another tank until radio contact was lost, when he was killed or mortally wounded by the enemy.*

Gregory's remains were returned to Vestal in 1948.

Charles J. Husted Jr.

Birth: October 21, 1921, Tarrytown, New York[345]
Death: January 11, 1946, Papua New Guinea
Burial: Lost at Sea; Memorialized at the Walls of the Missing at the Manilla American Cemetery, Philippines

Charles Husted graduated from North Tarrytown High School before enrolling at Colgate University, where he stayed for three years before entering the navy in 1942.[346] While at Colgate, he took flight training, and after he entered the navy, he took additional training in Chapel Hill, North Carolina; Lambert Field in St. Louis, Missouri; and in Pensacola, Florida, where he was commissioned an ensign.[347] He was serving as a pilot on the ship USS *Bunker Hill* in November 1943.[348] On November 11, 1943, Husted went missing after a mission. He was formally announced as deceased on January 11, 1946. In an article in February that year, insight into his passing was given, as told from a book on the USS *Bunker Hill*:

> *On the eve of his last mission over Rabaul, the young fighter pilot stood up to give his buddies a toast, expressing hope that they would all come back to talk it over. The entire squdron returned with the exception of Husted whos plane was last seen as it capitulated down in flames while he parachuted in the midst of strafing Japs.*
>
> *Before he met his fate Husted strafed several enemy ships, but as the squdron started back to its base enemy fighters appeared. Because of his wing position young Husted flew out to protect his squadron. He was alone in the plane with six machine guns to handle.*
>
> *Husted's commanding officer informed the family that that his actions at Rabaul was one of the turning points of the war. The planes that returned from Husted's fatal mission were so badly shot up that they had to be tossed into the sea.*[349]

PAUL C. MACDONALD JR.

Birth: January 13, 1921, Minneapolis, Minnesota[350]
Death: August 1, 1944, Tinian Island[351]
Burial: National Memorial Cemetery of the Pacific, Hawaii

Paul MacDonald graduated from Roosevelt High School in Yonkers in 1939. He enrolled at Colgate University and graduated in December 1943. Shortly after graduation, he enrolled in the Marine Corps and was commissioned a second lieutenant in early 1944. He trained in San Diego, California, and Hawaii before serving in the Pacific Theater. MacDonald was killed in action while attempting to save a wounded comrade during a battle on Tinian Island. He posthumously received a Silver Star for his actions that day:

> [F]*or conspicuous gallantry and intrepidity while attached to the Third Battalion, Eighth Marines, Second Marine Division, in action against*

enemy Japanese forces on Tinian Marianas Islands, 1 August 1944. Halted by fierce Japanese machine-gun and rifle fire while leading his platoon, Second Lieutenant MacDonald unhesitatingly risked his life in a daring attempt to save a seriously wounded Marine who was lying helpless in the line of enemy fire and, although struck by hostile bullets several times as he crossed the open field, valiantly persisted in his heroic effort until he fell, mortally wounded. By his resolute initiative, cool courage and self-sacrificing conduct on behalf of another, Second Lieutenant MacDonald was an inspiration to his men and upheld the highest traditions of the United States Navel Service. He gallantly gave his life for his country.

CLAYTON C. MCCLINTOCK

Birth: November 6, 1908, Franklin, New York[352]
Death: January 31, 1945, USS *Nevada*
Burial: Hillington Cemetery, Morris, New York

Clayton McClintock graduated from Franklin High School and operated the McClintock Dry Cleaning Service of Hamilton and Norwich. He married Marjorie Fay of New Berlin on September 24, 1944. McClintock joined the U.S. Naval Reserve in September 1942. He received his training at Great Lakes Naval Training Station, Illinois. He was assigned to the USS *Nevada* as a turret gunner in October 1942 and took part in the invasion of the Aleutians, Normandy, North Africa, Salerno and Southern France. McClintock died because of an accident aboard the USS *Nevada*. Clayton's father received a letter from Captain H.L. Grosskopf, commanding officer of the *Nevada*, dated February 8, 1945:

It is with deep regret that I write you regarding the death of your son Clayton Charles McClintock.

On January 31, 1945 at about 2:04 pm your son, while in the performance of his duty was mortally injured. He was carried immediately to the ship's hospital by his associates where he was given prompt medical attention by the ship's doctor who assured me that your son suffered no pain and that death was instantaneous.

During the time, your son served aboard this ship he made many friends among the officers and crew. His conduct was excellent and at the time of his death he was on the waiting list for promotion to Gunner's Mate third class.

He had been commended by his Commanding Officer for his courage and devotion to duty during the invasions of Normandy and Southern France, and the bombardment of Cherbourg.

On February 1st, funeral services were held on board with the entire ship's company, including myself and my officers, attending. The body was then sent ashore and interred with full military honors. Considerations of security prevent my disclosing the place of interment at this time but you will no doubt be furnished this information by the Navy Department when security permits.

In closing I wish to extend to you my deepest sympathy and to say that the death of your son is a distinct loss to the Navy and this ship.[353]

McClintock's remains were returned in 1948.

DENNIS J. MCDONALD

Birth: January 5, 1915, Hamilton, New York[354]
Death: March 13, 1945, Germany
Burial: St. Joseph's Cemetery, Hamilton, New York

Dennis McDonald attended local schools before joining the army in February 1942. He trained at Fort Benning in Georgia, Fort Jackson in South Carolina, Camp Blanding in Florida, Camp Forrest in Tennessee and Camp Atterbury in Indiana. Following training, he was sent overseas as a member of the 117th Infantry in February 1944. He received a Purple Heart for an injury that he suffered in France in July 1944. He rejoined his unit that November and was killed in action in Germany. His remains were returned home in November 1948.[355]

MARSH W. MILLER JR.

Birth: September 26, 1913[356]
Death: December 27, 1941, Philippines
Burial: Colgate University Cemetery, Hamilton, New York

Marsh Miller graduated from Binghamton Central School in 1933.[357] He enrolled at Colgate University and graduated in 1937. In July 1937, he enrolled in Naval Aviation School and was commissioned an ensign in December 1938. Shortly after receiving his commission, Miller married Miss Helen Johnson. In May 1941, Miller published an article entitled "Ferry Hop" in *Flying and Popular Aviation*.[358] The article talked about his transfer to VP-26 (Patrol Squadron 26) to ferry planes from the Naval Air Station at Pearl Harbor to Cavite. From there, he was assigned to the pioneer patrol squadron in the Asiatic Fleet. Shortly after he arrived for this assignment, his wife came to live with him at Cavite Naval Base in the Philippines until November 1940, when all wives and children were sent home. In January 1942, his family received notice that Miller was missing:

> *The Navy Department deeply regrets to inform you that your husband Ensign Marsh Weston Miller, Jr., US Naval Reserve, is missing, result of an air engagement with the enemy in performance of duty in the service of his country.*
>
> *The department appreciates your great anxiety and will furnish you further information when received.*
>
> *To prevent possible aid to the enemy, do not divulge the name of his ship or station.*[359]

In November 1945, the family received word that Miller was killed in action during an air attack in the Philippines.[360] According to the report:

> *Miller gave his life on December 27, 1941 when his plane was shot down by enemy aircraft fire during an attack on Japanese shipping in the harbor of Jolo Sulu Provence....* [T]*he attack was not only successful from a military standpoint, but proved to be an inspiration to Moro natives who have commemorated this action in ballads and acclaiming the bravery of American fliers.*

In May 1949, his remains were returned to the United States.[361]

PHIL R. MILLER

Birth: February 1920, Detroit, Michigan[362]
Death: January 11, 1944, Germany[363]
Burial: Arlington National Cemetery, Virginia

Shortly after his birth, Phil Miller's family moved to Penn Yan, where he attended Penn Yan Academy before transferring to Greenbrier Military School in Lewisburg, West Virginia. Following his graduation, he enrolled at Colgate University, graduating in 1941. He then took a position with the National City Bank in New York City before joining the U.S. Army Air Corps in March 1942. Miller received training as a navigator at Maxwell Field in Alabama, Selman Field in Louisiana and in Kearney, Nebraska. He was sent overseas to the European Theater and was killed when his plane crashed. One of the survivors of the crash, Staff Sergeant Bernard Keene, gave the family an account of what happened.[364] Their B-17 Flying Fortress

> *was attacked on the way to the target which was in Oschersleben, Germany. They fought desperately for more than half an hour without help, having been forced out of formation. The Ball turret was shot off with the gunner in it, the bombardier was killed and the tail was shot off and the tail gunner killed. The Fortress went into a spin, exploded and broke in two. The front half, with Lieutenant Miller and five other crew members in it, hurtled to the ground, crashed and burned. The tail half, being lighter leveled off and sent down more slowly giving the two waist gunners, the only two left alive in that part, a chance to bail out…*
>
> *The officers and men in the front of the Fortress never had a chance to save themselves after the plane went into the spin. Upon being asked why the whole crew did not bail out earlier the Staff Sergeant replied that they were too busy fighting trying to get back into the formation and proceed to the target to even think about it.*

Miller's remains were returned in 1951.[365]

William S. Rising III

Birth: January 29, 1920, Brooklyn, New York[366]
Death: September 4, 1945, Wyoming[367]
Burial: Woodlawn Cemetery, Bronxville, New York

William Rising graduated from Erasmus Hall High School and enrolled at Colgate University. It was at a Colgate University social event in Hamilton where he met his future wife, Virginia Miller. He left Colgate to take a job at the American Tobacco Company while taking night classes at St. John's University. Rising enlisted in the navy in 1942 and trained as a pilot. Following his training, he married Miller in June 1943, and they had one daughter, Susan. He served in the Pacific Theater and received numerous medals, including the Navy Cross and the Distinguished Flying Cross for his actions over Manilla in the fall of 1944.[368] The citation for the Navy Cross reads:

> [F]*or extraordinary heroism in operations against the enemy while serving as a Pilot of a carrier-based Navy Dive Bomber in Bombing Squadron 15, attached to the USS Essex in action against enemy Japanese surface forces in the vicinity of the Philippine Islands during the Battle of Leyte Gulf on 25 October 1944. Fearlessly pressing home his attack to low altitude in the face of accurate and intense anti-aircraft fire from the formidable enemy disposition, Lieutenant, Junior Grade, Rising succeeded in scoring one of the eight direct hits upon a Japanese aircraft carrier of Chitose class, in a strike so effectively disposed that the resulting successive hits upon this ship caused its almost immediate sinking. Undaunted in the face of relentless, devastating anti-aircraft fire, he rendered gallant service during the bitterly fought engagement in which all carriers, a light cruiser and a destroyer of the enemy's task force were sunk and heavy bomb and torpedo damage inflicted on battleships and other important naval units. By his daring airmanship, exceptional courage and steadfast devotion to duty through a perilous assignment, Lieutenant, Junior Grade, Rising contributed materially to the sinking of this valuable enemy fighting unit and upheld the highest traditions of the United States Naval Service.*[369]

He received the Distinguished Flying Cross for aiding in the sinking of a Japanese battleship during the battle of the Philippines.[370] He was declared missing in action after his plane was shot down on Luzon. The account of his survival states:

> *He was shot down over Manilla, crash-landing in the sea near an uninhabited island off Corregidor. He lived on the island with his Kentucky-born gunner for two days, existing on crabs and snails, while Jap dive-bombers strafed the small piece of land. Then the two hoisted sail on a rubber boat and made their way to Mindoro. Two Yank PT boats dashing through Mindoro Strait several weeks later picked up the Brooklynite and his gunner who paddled out to meet the craft.*

He returned home after his efforts and was assigned to West Virginia and then Oregon.[371] When he was in Oregon, Virginia and Susan moved out to be with Rising. After receiving a leave in anticipation of his discharge, the family packed up their vehicle and headed east. In Newcastle, Wyoming, both rear tires of the sedan blew out, causing the car to overturn. Both William and Virginia died at the hospital shortly after the accident. Susan was unharmed in the accident.

Thomas L. Rockwell

Birth: May 14, 1923, Wellsboro, Pennsylvania[372]
Death: December 24, 1944, Belgium
Burial: Henry-Chappelle American Cemetery and Memorial, Belgium; Memorialized Wellsboro Cemetery, Pennsylvania

Thomas Rockwell graduated from Wellsboro High School in June 1940. He studied at Colgate University for a year before studying at Dickinson College and Mansfield State Teachers College. He left school and joined the U.S. Army Air Corps in April 1942. He was classified as a pilot, took preflight training at Kelly Field in Texas, flight training at Samford-Arledge Field in Texas and advanced flight training at Goodfellow Field in Texas. Following his flight training, he attended officer training school in the infantry and trained at Fort Benning in Georgia. He was commissioned a lieutenant in November 1943. He continued training and worked as an instructor before he attended paratrooper school at Fort Benning. He received the wings and boots of a paratrooper in June 1944. Following completion, he toured with a group of paratroopers doing exhibition jumps to promote the fifth war loan. He wrote of one his tour experiences in New York City:

> *I had an exciting time jumping over Mitchell Field. I was in No. 1 position and pushed out an equipment parapack, then ran back to No. 16 position and followed the stick out, whirling around the sky with a Mae West life preserver on plus reserve chute, field pack, 3x4 foot map, board with maps and aerial photos, canteen, Garand rifle (11 pounds), ammunition, grenades, K ration, shaving kit, first aid packet and the kitchen sink! By the time the 16 of us got out, the plane was past the field and I was whirling around in a terrific wind; I had to spill my chute to keep from hitting electric wires and slipped between them, over a house, avoiding two macadam roads. I dropped plop into a back yard where a woman holding a six months old baby saw me land. She began screaming and soon the whole street full of back yards was filled with hysterical and frightened women yelling, "Look at the German Paratrooper." They thought I was a Nazi and it's a wonder I wasn't riddled with bullets. I was yards from nowhere and nothing around but a 75 mm howitzer, which the artillery had dropped. All alone in a Long Island village. My face was all puffed up and bleeding from the rifle which banged and mashed up my face on the opening shock. Women, little girls and babies were all screaming around me, but I didn't have time to explain as I had to run with full pack to the rendezvous a mile away. What a show, I really should have broken my neck but I managed to keep my wits and everything is ok.*[373]

He was sent overseas initially to England in August 1944 before being sent to the European mainland. He was killed in action in Belgium when his unit dropped behind German lines during the Battle of the Bulge.[374]

Frederick N. Sinclair

Birth: February 22, 1918, Earlville, New York[375]
Death: December 16, 1943, Italy
Burial: Sicily-Rome American Cemetery & Memorial, Italy

Frederick Sinclair graduated from Earlville Central Schools and then attended the Morrisville Agricultural School. Sinclair married Virginia Brocker of Waterville in July 1941, and they had a son, Frederick Douglas, in 1942. Prior to the war, he was working as the manager of a gasoline station in Auburn, New York. He was inducted into the army in August 1941. He received training at Fort Niagara in New York, Fort Eustis in Virginia, Fort Michie in New York, Camp Walters in Texas and Camp Swift in Texas. He then attended Officers' Training School in Fort Benning Georgia, graduating in December 1942. Sinclair was killed in action in Italy on December 16, 1943. He was posthumously awarded the Presidential Citation for Meritorious Conduct and a Purple Heart.

Ernest S. Spurling

Birth: December 8, 1917, Tennessee[376]
Death: March 30, 1943, Tunisia
Burial: West Eaton Cemetery, New York

Earnest Spurling moved with his mom and siblings to the town of Hamilton between 1935 and 1940.[377] Prior to the war, Spurling worked at a number of farms in Madison and Chenango Counties as a laborer. He enlisted in the army in October 1940. Spurling trained at Fort Niagara in New York and in Virginia, North Carolina and Massachusetts. He was sent to England in April 1942, and he took part in the North African invasion. He was killed in action near Tunisia.

Robert Soule Swan

Birth: December 30, 1918, Amsterdam, New York[378]
Death: July 27, 1943, New York[379]
Burial: Remains Not Recovered; Memorialized at East Coast Memorial, Manhattan, New York

Upon graduation of high school, Robert Swan enlisted at Colgate University, graduating in 1941. While at Colgate, he took part in Civilian Pilot Training's private and secondary courses. He joined the Naval Reserve and was commissioned a lieutenant. He was cited for Navy Decoration for his assistance in sinking an Axis U-boat in 1943. According to accounts:

> *He crawled from the bombardier's blister of the Catalina flying boat to release the explosives which sent the U-Boat to the bottom…*

> *Hidden by the Haze, the PBY which Lieutenant Swan was flying caught the U-Boat cruising on the surface with many of its crew on the deck, apparently sun bathing.*

In an article in the *St. Petersburg (FL) Times*, Swan was quoted as saying:

> *I guess the splash of the waves drowned the noise of our motors until we were almost over the target.…I had a good look at the men on the deck and they certainly were startled to see us. Some just stood there as if frozen in fear. A couple I believe threw their hands over their heads. Then suddenly they ran toward the conning tower and tried to scramble in. The sub was about to dive and leave them, I guess.*

He was declared missing in action in July 1943 when his plane crashed off the coast of New York City. He was posthumously awarded the Distinguished Flying Cross for his actions on the day he disappeared:[380]

> *Swan rendered invaluable assistance to his bomber pilot fighting an enemy submarine until one of the bombs released from his plane destroyed the vessel and sent his own damaged aircraft plunging into the sea.*

Charles W. Tribken Jr.

Birth: July 29, 1918, Rochester, New York[381]
Death: November 22, 1944, France[382]
Burial: Long Island National Cemetery, East Farmingdale, New York

Charles Tribken Jr. grew up in Rochester and later Brooklyn, graduating from Erasmus Hall High School in 1936. He studied geology for three years at Colgate University before enrolling in flight training at Floyd Bennett Field in Brooklyn, New York. He was later transferred to the Pensacola Naval Flying School. After completing the flying school, Tribken continued his studies at the University of California, leaving to enroll in the Polaris Flying School in Glendale, California. In April 1941, he joined the British Royal Air Force. Newspapers reported that Tribken took part in multiple raids in Sicily and France, as well as fighting off large formations of enemy bombers in Malta.[383] He transferred to the U.S. Army in January 1942.[384] He was credited with shooting down three planes in the Royal Air Force and received a commendation from the British government for blowing up a locomotive in France. He worked as an instructor in combat flying before requesting to be reassigned to the European Theater in 1944.[385] Tribken talked about some of experiences while home in February 1943:

> *I respect the Italian pilots more than the Germans. They will follow through in a fight where the Germans run away. The Italians have a swell new plane, the Macchi 202. It's as good as the Messerschmitt 109, but I don't think it will be much of a danger to us because the Italians can't produce enough of them...*[386]
>
> *Just in case anyone doesn't think that war bonds are terribly important, let them think this over. When you don't get the goods you need, you can't go on feeling you're not licked.*
>
> *The Allied pilots are much better than the Germans, but what we needed to make the battle even was planes as good as theirs, faster planes, with more climb and chiefly more of them. That's the answer in a nutshell—more planes. It still is the answer.*[387]

He was killed in Toule, France, when the vehicle he was traveling in accidently went over the edge of a cliff. Tribken's remains were returned home in 1948.

Robert Waghorn

Birth: July 26, 1915, East Hamilton, New York[388]
Death: January 23, 1943, Manitoba[389]
Burial: Earlville Cemetery, New York

Robert Waghorn grew up in East Hamilton and Sherburne. Waghorn married Emma Moon in June 1942; they had a son, Robert Douglas.[390] Prior to enlisting, he worked as a laborer and truck driver.[391] Waghorn was inducted in March 1941. He trained at Madison Barracks and Pine Camp in New York, Fort Ethan Allen in Vermont, Camp Bragg in North Carolina and the Aberdeen Proving Grounds in Maryland.[392] He was selected to test heavy artillery in subzero temperatures at Camp Shilo in Manitoba. He died at Camp Shilo after contracting pneumonia.

LEBANON

Eugene J. Parteko

Birth: October 7, 1917, Toole, Utah[393]
Death: October 31, 1944, France[394]
Burial: Epinal American Cemetery and Memorial, France; Memorial at Eaton Village Cemetery, New York

Eugene Parteko was born in Utah before spending most of his youth growing up in Lebanon, New York.[395] He volunteered for the army infantry in November 1940 and trained in Washington, Louisiana, North and South Carolina and Camp Chaffee in Arkansas. He was sent to England in 1942 and took part in the invasion of France. Parteko was killed in action.

Fred Riggalls

Birth: January 9, 1914, Georgetown, New York[396]
Death: March 29, 1945, Germany[397]
Burial: Netherlands American Cemetery and Memorial, Netherlands; Memorial at Hillside Cemetery, Georgetown, New York

Fred Riggalls grew up in Lebanon and was in New Jersey when he was drafted into the army in January 1941. After training at Fort Bragg in North Carolina, he was sent to England in January 1943. He served in North Africa and Sicily before returning to England and taking part in the invasion of France. He was wounded in action near Normandy in August 1944 and received the Purple Heart. He returned to action in October and served until he was killed in action near the Rhine River in Germany.

LENOX

Philip Wayne Ackerman

Birth: June 18, 1923, Whitelaw, New York[398]
Death: November 13, 1942
Burial: Lost at Sea; Memorials at the Whitelaw Cemetery, Lenox, New York; Tablet of the Missing, Manila American Cemetery and Memorial, Philippines

Philip Ackerman went to local Canastota schools and excelled in football and wrestling. Following his graduation in 1941, he went to work at Oneida Limited but enlisted in the navy the day after the Japanese attack on Pearl Harbor in December 1941.[399] He trained in Newport, Rhode Island, and served in the Pacific. He was killed in the Guadalcanal area. In March 1944, his family received a Purple Heart medal. His remains were not located.

Image taken from the Kenwood Chronicle. *Courtesy of the Oneida Community Mansion House.*

Joseph Buda

Birth: February 28, 1919, Canastota, New York[400]
Death: September 17, 1944, Italy
Burial: Long Island National Cemetery, East Farmingdale, New York

Joseph Buda attended local schools and worked as a member of the local police department. Prior to the war, he married Elsie Brooks, a teacher, and they had a daughter. He joined the service in early 1942 and trained in Mississippi, California and New Jersey before going overseas in December 1943. He first went to Africa and then Italy. Shortly before his family received the telegram of his death, one of his sisters received a letter from him explaining that he was in Florence, Italy, and that at the pace they were going he would be home soon. He was killed in action in Italy.

Charles W. Cordell

Birth: March 5, 1925, Clockville, New York[401]
Death: September 26, 1944, Holland
Burial: Arlington National Cemetery, Virginia

Following the death of his mother around 1930, Charles Cordell and his sister lived with his Aunt Elizabeth of Oneida.[402] Prior to the war, Cordell was working at the Queensboro Farm Products Company in Canastota.[403] Cordell entered the service around 1942 and trained as a paratrooper at Camp Croft, South Carolina, and Fort Benning, Georgia. He was seriously wounded while landing in Holland on September 20, 1944, and he died six days later. His remains were returned home in 1948.

George C. Cox

Birth: October 13, 1921, Verona Station, New York[404]
Death: May 12, 1944, Italy[405]
Burial: Mount Pleasant Cemetery, Canastota, New York

George Cox graduated from Canastota High School. Following graduation, Cox worked at the Lee Manufacturing Company and the A&P Store in

Canastota. He enlisted in July 1942. He trained in Oklahoma; Shreveport, Louisiana; and San Antonio, Texas, before being deployed overseas in November 1943. He was promoted to staff sergeant while at Camp Gruber in Oklahoma in April 1943.[406] In April 1944, Cox took part in the capture of two German snipers.[407] This event was recounted first in the *St. Louis Globe-Democrat* and later in local newspapers:

> *With the Fifth Army, Italy—The smell of rankish cigarette smoke recently resulted in capture of two German soldiers on the Fifth Army front in Italy by a 10-man infantry patrol led by Technical Sergeant George C. Cox of Canastota, NY.*
>
> *The patrol had gone deep into enemy lines during the night and waited until about 10 in the morning, when Germans would likely be asleep, before dashing into heavily fortified German positions to make the capture Cox related.*
>
> *The patrol leader called for artillery fire on a building where Germans were thought to be staying and as they raced for the building under protection of Fifth Army artillery shells he said he "smelled a rankish tobacco." Closer investigation revealed a well camouflaged foxhole where two Nazi soldiers were smoking cigarettes.*
>
> *A couple of us stuck our guns in and motioned for them to come out with their hands up. One came out willingly but the other was reluctant.*
>
> *The one who had come out pleaded for the other one to come out also. Finally he did, but just about the time Germans on another section of the hill fired rifles at us.*
>
> *The patrol took the best cover afforded, keeping the prisoners under guard and a little while later crawled into a stream which led back to the Fifth Army Lines, about two miles away.*
>
> *While in the stream the patrol was subject to heavy German artillery and mortar fire and was pinned down several hours before it could start back to the Fifth Army Lines, Cox said.*[408]

Shortly after this action, Cox was promoted to technical sergeant. One month later, he was killed in action in Italy. Cox's remains were brought home in 1948.

FRANKLIN WARD DAVIDSON

Birth: March 19, 1907, Cortland, New York[409]
Death: April 12, 1944, Italy
Burial: Mount Pleasant Cemetery, Canastota, New York

Franklin Davidson graduated from Canastota High School in 1924 and later attended the Mechanics Institute in Rochester, New York, graduating in 1930. He married Kathryn Davis of Rochester in November 1929. Following his marriage, he worked at E.W. Edwards & Son in Rochester, before returning to Central New York to work at Onondaga Floors of Syracuse in 1937. He entered the army in January 1943 and was trained as a military police officer at Fort Riley, Kansas, and in Greenville, Pennsylvania. He went overseas in June 1943 and spent time in North Africa and Italy. He was promoted to corporal in March 1944. In a letter to his wife published in January 1944, Davidson talked about his experiences:

> *At last I can tell you that I have moved, and generally where I am. You can imagine how difficult it has been to write, not being able to say we had moved or where we were, as the only things we have to write about revolve around these topics.*
>
> *We have found a climate here quite like ours at home. It is a blessed relief from the terrible heat we endured in Africa. For the first time since leaving the states I have seen the seen civilization as we know it, especially in the metropolitan centers.*
>
> *The damage and suffering here has been great, as you know from your papers and radio. The people are kind, friendly and warm-hearted. As is true wherever the American soldier goes, he makes a great hit with his candy and cigarettes which he shares generously with the people. They are crazy about these things.*
>
> *Everywhere we go they think the Americans are all rich. They are greatly impressed by our wealth and might as manifested by the fabulous supplies pouring into the country.*
>
> *Most of the people here are of light complexion and blondes and red heads are not uncommon. They are delighted by the quick manner in which we pick up and use words and phrases of their language and enthusiastically and patiently teach us to talk with them. One man told me the Italians like and respect the Americans and did not wish the war with us but were forced into it. However, for the time being we are reserving our opinion on this matter. He said that they have had much trouble and the loss of children was great.*

The universal confection here and the only one is a nut bar made of nuts and molasses. Everyone eats it and we go for it strong. It is sold in stores, on the streets, at stands and by vendors everywhere. Food of course is very scarce. There are some apples, potatoes and nuts similar to our English walnuts that we devour by the kilo. There are lots of persimmons and soon oranges and lemons will be ripe.

This is a beautiful and scenic country. I have walked in streets nearly 2000 years old and it gives me a sensation difficult to express. I have seen sights that ordinarily only the wealthy tourist could enjoy. I now appreciate that this country is the seat of an old and great civilization of the arts.[410]

Less than three months after this letter was published, Davidson was killed in action on the Anzio beachhead in Italy when he was struck by an enemy shell while checking the guard.[411]

Dominic DiVencenzo

Birth: April 18, 1909, Canastota, New York[412]
Death: September 20, 1944, Italy
Burial: St. Agatha Cemetery, Canastota, New York

Dominic DiVencenzo (also DeVincenzo or DiVincenzo) graduated from local schools and was working at the New York Central Freight House in Utica, New York, prior to his entering the service. He was married to the former Mary Aiello of Utica. He joined the army around January 1944 and trained at Camp Croft in South Carolina before being sent overseas to Italy. He was shot and killed in action during the invasion of Italy.

Clarence D. Farrington

Birth: Around 1917, New York[413]
Death: March 6, 1944, Holland[414]
Burial: Ardennes American Cemetery and Memorial, Belgium

Clarence Farrington graduated from Canastota High School and worked as a farm laborer and at New Process Gear before enlisting in July 1940. He went to Oklahoma for basic training before attending additional training at

Victory Field in Texas. He obtained his pilot's wings after training at Twin Engine Bomber Training school in Pampa, Texas, in June 1943. He was sent overseas in December of that year. He was originally listed as a prisoner of war after his plane was forced to land in Holland on March 6, 1944.[415] It was later reported that the plane he was in was blown up midair over Bentheim, Germany.[416] He was posthumously awarded the Purple Heart.[417]

Carroll (Carl) R. Hayden

Birth: November 24, 1916, Hopkinton, New York[418]
Death: May 29, 1944, England
Burial: Cambridge American Cemetery and Memorial, Cambridgeshire, England

Carroll Hayden's family moved to Canastota, and he attended and graduated from local schools. Following graduation, he worked at the Cunningham Ice Company, Buyea's Market and later the Rome Air Depot.[419] In September 1940, he married Margaret Tailby of Minoa, New York. Hayden entered the field artillery in February 1943 and trained at Fort Bragg in North Carolina before being sent to the Mediterranean and later England. He was killed in Barton Stacy, England.[420] A letter to Hayden's wife from Major General J.A. Ulio explained what happened:

> *This report disclosed that Pvt. Hayden died almost instantly on the night of May 28th, 1944 as a result of injuries sustained when he was accidentally struck by a projection on a truck while walking along the Bullington Cross–Andover Rd. near Barton Stacy, England.*
>
> *Medical Aid was summoned but death occurred before your husband could be removed to a hospital, Pvt. Hayden was on an authorized pass at the time of the accident.*

Lyle C. Hendrickson

Birth: July 5, 1922, Antwerp, New York[421]
Death: January 16, 1944, Italy[422]
Burial: Mount Pleasant Cemetery, Canastota, New York

Lyle Hendrickson grew up in the town of Lenox, and following high school, he worked for the New York Central Railroad in Syracuse and later as a farmhand for A. Fisher & Sons in Canastota. He entered the army in March 1943 and trained at Fort McClelland in Alabama before going overseas in July.[423] In a letter to his family from November 1943, he wrote about fighting along the Italian coast:

> *When we hit the beach it looked like the Fourth of July. I always did like the pretty red colors, but I don't think I like them anymore they have too much of a whine when they come close.*
>
> *You've probably heard about the German gun called the 88. It shoots a projectile about four or five inches long and two and a half in diameter. These projectiles whistle when they go over your head.*
>
> *Four of us fellows were sitting by our fox holes when all of a sudden something went whistling by. One of us said I think that's an 88. You know how woodchucks jump into their holes when they see you? Well that's just how we four looked diving back into our fox holes. We have to sit back now and laugh about times like these. The Jerries aren't so very tough as one may think. I guess I know how to get a Jerry before he gets me.*[424]

Hendrickson was killed instantly near San Angelo, Italy. A letter received from Brigadier General Robert H. Dunlop explained what happened:

> *Your desire to learn the details of the circumstances attending your son's death is fully appreciated and a report has now been received in this office which states that Private Hendrickson was killed in action in the vicinity of San Angelo, Italy on 16 January 1944. The report further discloses that your son was occupying a foxhole when struck by a shell fragment which killed him instantly. It is not expected that further reports will be received in the War Department concerning your son but should additional information become available it will be forwarded to you promptly.*[425]

The family received an additional letter in 1945 from 141st Infantry chaplain Charles A. Francis:

> *Time that has elapsed since the death of your son has pressed deeply into my mind and heart, the fact that this supreme sacrifice was made that others might live. He fought with a strong faith in God and his fellow soldiers. He fell that our cause of right might continue. I assure you that my thoughts*

> *and prayers shall continue to follow you each day. May your courage in continuing to bear your bereavement be as great as that of Lyle in the performance of his duty.*
>
> *As chaplain of the battalion to which PFC Hendrickson was assigned at the time of his death I am writing to offer my sympathy. Lyle paid the great price that we as a free people might continue to enjoy the things of life that are worthwhile. By that he willingly did his job well which has inspired other men to follow his example and has expressed his intense love for us. Greater love than this no man hath, that a man lay down his life for his friend. Thus we are greatly indebted to him to such extent that we can never repay but rather live in the spirit of his courage. Surely God in His Infinite mercy has given him the reward he so well deserves.*[426]

He was posthumously awarded the Purple Heart.[427] In October 1943, his brother Cyril, a member of the 3rd Regiment State Guard in Oneida, was killed in a car accident while returning home from drill.[428]

VINCENT LOMONACO

Birth: June 13, 1925, Canastota, New York[429]
Death: October 30, 1944, Italy[430]
Burial: Florence American Cemetery and Memorial, Italy

Vincent Lomonaco attended local schools and worked at the Parkell Drug Company before joining the army in November 1943. He trained at Camp Upton in New York, Camp Shelby in Mississippi and then at Fort Meade in Maryland. Lomanaco was sent to Italy in July 1944. While in Italy, he wrote to his parents in October 1944:

> *Just came back from chow and remembered I had to write a letter and enclose a couple of pictures I had taken in Naples. It was a rainy day and I look kind of sloppy. I had a swell dinner and supper.*
>
> *I went to an old castle overlooking all Naples. It was a swell view. I went thru an old monastery which was 600 years old and the paintings still look like new. Some of them looked just like statues but were only paint. There were also some old boats and two horse drawn carriages. One was solid gold. The king used to ride in it.*

> *I got up to this place in a cable car which went up at about a 30 degree angle under buildings that were on the side of the mountain. It seemed like the subway only a lot slower.*[431]

Less than a month later, his family received word that Lomonaco was killed in action in northern Italy after being struck by artillery.

Anthony (Antonio) Maula

Birth: July 21, 1923, Italy[432]
Death: December 15, 1944, Florida
Burial: St. Agatha's Cemetery, Canastota, New York

Anthony Maula's family came to the United States when he was around five years old. He graduated from Canastota High School in 1941. He attended the National Defense Aviation School in Syracuse and was working at Rome Air Field as a mechanic prior to his enlistment.[433] He enlisted in the U.S. Army Air Corps in February 1942.[434] He trained at Maxwell Field in Alabama, Cochran Field in Georgia and Napier Field in Alabama. He was stationed at Sarasota Army Airbase when he was killed in an airplane accident.

Burton Cardner Middleditch

Birth: September 2, 1926, Canastota, New York[435]
Death: November 30, 1944, Hawaii
Burial: Lenox Rural Cemetery, Canastota, New York

Burton Middleditch attended local schools before enlisting in the Marine Corps in September 1943. He went to basic training at Parris Island, South Carolina, training as an engineer. Middleditch was assigned to Company A, 4th Engineering Battalion, 4th Marine Division, Fleet Marine Force. He received additional training at Camp Lejeune in North Carolina and in Quantico, Virginia.[436] On July 7, 1944, Middleditch married Helen Wanamaker of Canastota.[437] He died while serving on the island of Maui in the Hawaiian Islands on November 30, 1944. Burton's remains were returned home in 1947.

Charles B. Narehood

Birth: May 10, 1922, Surveyor, Pennsylvania[438]
Death: July 31, 1945, France
Burial: Remains Not Found; Memorialized at Brittany American Cemetery and Memorial, France

Charles Narehood graduated from Verona High School in 1938. The family moved to Canastota following his graduation.[439] He enlisted in the army in October 1940.[440] Two brothers, William (meteorologist) and Carl (corporal), served in the army, as did brother-in-law Harold Gondrez, who was in the U.S. Army Air Corps. Charles trained at Fort Monmouth in New Jersey with a signal repair company. He transferred to the air corps and trained as a pilot in Selma, Alabama. He was commissioned a lieutenant in April 1943. In October 1943, he was sent overseas. In March 1944, Narehood was awarded an Air Medal. He was declared missing in action on July 30, 1944. In January 1945, he was awarded the Silver Star for gallantry and an Oak Leaf Cluster. (He was later awarded three additional Oak Leaf Clusters.) The citation for the Silver Star reads:

> *For gallantry in action July 30th, 1944. On this date Lt. Narehood led a flight of P-47 type aircraft in an attack upon a special military installation which impeded the advance of an Allied armored column.*
>
> *Upon its arrival at the target area, the flight encountered an intense barrage of anti-aircraft fire. Poor visibility necessitated that the attack be executed at extremely low level.*
>
> *With full knowledge of the great hazard involved in flying through the strong enemy fire, Lt. Narehood gallantly led his flight to the target area and despite severe damage to his aircraft, successfully directed the operations of his flight until after his plane had four times been struck by anti-aircraft fire, he was forced to crash land in enemy territory.*[441]

Narehood was declared dead in August 1945, with a listed death date as July 31, 1944. His death notice states:

> *His plane, damaged by anti-aircraft fire while engaged in a ground support mission was seen to crash land in a field northwest of Percy, France, 15 miles from St. Lo.*

FRANK PENNA

Birth: January 21, 1919, Canastota, New York[442]
Death: November 20, 1943, Gilbert Islands
Burial: St. Agatha's Cemetery, Canastota, New York

Frank Penna attended Canastota High School and worked on his family's farm prior to the war. He enlisted in the U.S. Marine Corps in April 1942.[443] He trained at Parris Island, South Carolina, and San Diego. He was killed in action on Tarawa in the Gilbert Islands.[444] Corporal Laurence A. Smith wrote to the family about what happened.

> *This letter is one of the hardest I have ever written in my life. First of all I'm Corporal Laurence A. Smith Sr. Perhaps your son Joe as we have all come to call him, has mentioned me in some of his letters home to you.*
>
> *I too must share your grief for since knowing your son, I have come to love him as much as I do my own brothers. It seems that we both had the same ear for music, dancing, etc. Always we would talk as to what we two would do when we returned to the states together.*
>
> *Joe or Frankie as you all must have called him at home was in my squad. Little Ferrone was his asst. sq. Leader. He also loved Joe, as the rest of the fellows in my sq, did. Little Ferrone told me upon my return from the hospital, that he had written to you. The reason for my delay in writing is that I had to be sure you had received word from DC. I also feel it is my duty to Joe, and because I loved him so much, I shall do the same.*
>
> *Joe never asked me to write in case of something unforeseen, which may happen. I am doing so anyway for there are many things I want to tell you which I feel you shall be happy to hear and may always hold in your hearts when your thoughts at moments become full of the many things you both loved so well in your son.*
>
> *On D Day, November 20th, my squad was split in two, with Little Ferrone taking one-half and I the other. Joe* [a nickname for Frank according to the letter] *was in the same track as I for he wanted it that way and so did I. We were side by side all the way into and on the beach until we were forced to part.*
>
> *When still 500 yards from the beach, the Japs opened fire with their 20 MM on our track and we were both quiet. While still 200 yards from the beach I turned and asked Joe, I said "Joe have you said a good Act of Contrition" and he answered, "Yes twice, have you?" I told him, always*

before something like this Joe. "May God Bless you" he said. Same from me to you and then we were on the beach.

Three of us were together, Joe, Horne and I. When I saw this Jap throw a grenade at us, I yelled grenade and the three of us dropped flat on deck but we were all wounded. Joe received a small piece just beside his nose, Horne in both legs, myself in the right leg, back and buttocks. Then all hell broke loose. We crawled up to the revetment where I left orders for Joe and Horne to stay put behind the revetment. Because it was the safest place on the island at the time and am sure all thru the whole 76 hours. So I left them there and happy in my heart that at least two of my boys were safe with only small wounds.

I was carried aboard ship on the 21st because of concussion received when only 3 yards from an ammunition dump which blew up. I had hopes and prayers that Joe would be on the same ship. At the hospital I asked if he was listed in any ward. So, I said a prayer that he was sent right to the states. It wasn't until I rejoined my unit here, three weeks ago that I found our Joe was buried on the Island of Tarawa, for which he gave his life so that his other shipmates could over-run.

Joe did not have to go any farther but could have stayed where I ordered him to. So please keep this thought "That your son died a hero" in my eyes the best one on the island. Yes, Joe is a hero and to us fellows who loved him, he shall never leave our minds. But always in future battles, he shall be alongside of us, to spur us on to try and do as well as he himself did. If that can be possible.

Mrs. Penna, when we threw our last liberty in New Zealand Joe loaned me $20 in American. I know you will not want this money so am taking it, I shall have a high mass said for Joe. I'm sure your son is in heaven with his, yours and my God, whom we all love unto death.

My one wish is that you and your husband and the rest of Joe's family shall be happy to know that Joe died a holy death, Such as he and I would choose.

Penna was posthumously awarded the Purple Heart. In 1949, his remains were declared non-recoverable; however, through the work of History Flight Inc., his remains were returned home in 2016 after they were located on Betio Island.[445]

Donald B. Roberts

Birth: September 17, 1921, New York[446]
Death: March 26, 1944, France
Burial: Henry-Chappelle American Cemetery and Memorial, Belgium; Memorial, Glenwood Cemetery, Oneida, New York

Donald Roberts graduated from Oneida High School and worked for CMC prior to the war. He was drafted and inducted into the U.S. Army Air Corps in July 1942.[447] He trained at Keesler Field, Mississippi, and Goering Aircraft School in Washington, D.C., and earned his silver wings after graduating from gunnery school in Las Vegas, Nevada. He had additional training at Ephrate and Geiger Field in Washington and Great Falls and Lewiston, Idaho. Roberts was sent overseas in October 1943. He was declared missing over France on March 26, 1944, when his plane failed to return from a mission. Later, it was confirmed that Roberts was killed when his plane was hit by flak and the bombs exploded.[448] Just prior to his disappearance, he was awarded the Air Medal with an Oak Leaf Cluster for completing fifteen missions.

Robert R. Sayers

Birth: June 21, 1910, Coxsackie-on-the-Hudson, New York[449]
Death: October 15, 1942, Guadalcanal
Burial: Lost at Sea; Wall of the Missing at the Manila American Cemetery, Philippines

Robert Sayers's family moved to Cazenovia when he was a small child and then to Canastota when he was around the age of six. Sayers graduated from Canastota High School in June 1931. Prior to his graduation, he took an aviation course at the Curtiss-Wright School in Syracuse and is believed to be the first resident of Canastota to obtain a private pilot's licenses. He enlisted in the navy in 1931 and trained in Newport, at the Great Lakes aviation mechanics school. In 1936, he married Helen Hagar of Norfolk, Virginia. Following his graduation from aviation school, Sayers continued to serve in the navy. In 1940, he was cited for perfect conduct, having never had a mark against him, an honor that he would have until the end of his life. At the outbreak of the war, Sayers was reassigned from Norfolk, Virginia, to Quonset Point, Rhode Island, and then he was sent to San Francisco, California, and on to Hawaii. Sayers served with Dighton Polan.[450] Polan flew in the same bombing mission as Sayers on October 15, 1942. Polan's parents relayed the following report from a Lieutenant Martin, who was acquainted with the events:

> *At dawn on the morning of October 15th, 1942, six bombers started out in fan like formations from a base in the far southwest pacific in search of the enemy. The sea was calm although clouds filled the skies. When they reached a certain point in their flight, they flew in different directions. Suddenly and without warming at 9 o'clock of that same morning, a Japanese Zero started out of a cloud and struck a direct hit on the bomber, which carried nine men, one of them my son. The bomber burst into flames. Even so, a radio message sounded "hit" almost to the last as the ship sank into the Pacific.*

Martin continued:

> *If he had not excelled in his line of duty he might have been alive today for Hawaii was his base but upon arriving in the southwest pacific, conditions at that early date were serious. Men and planes were scarce. Due to these conditions, a list of the best men in their positions was made out and on that list was the name of Robert R. Sayers, A.C.M.M.* [Aviation Chief Machinist's Mate]. *These men stayed to meet the enemy in the air.*

Sayers was the first man from Canastota killed in action during World War II.

Carmen T. Tornatore

Birth: Around 1925, New York[451]
Death: March 15, 1945, France[452]
Burial: Ardennes American Cemetery and Memorial, Belgium

Carmen Tornatore graduated from Canastota High School in 1942 and enlisted in the army during the same year. He was originally reported missing in action in December 1944. In February 1945, a letter confirmed that he was a prisoner. He was somehow able to return to his line.[453] He was killed at Niederbronn, France, while leading a group of five volunteers to break up a German ambush with hand grenades.[454] They were killed by a machine gunner after completing the mission.

Vincent W. Walters

Birth: October 25, 1922, Dansville, New York[455]
Death: June 9, 1944, France[456]
Burial: Sunnyside Cemetery, Lincoln, New York

Vincent Walters graduated from Oneida High School, and prior to the war, he was working as a farmer.[457] Walters enlisted in the army in July 1942.[458] He trained in the Signal Corps at Fort Benning in Georgia and Fort Knox in Kentucky before going to England in January 1944. While in England, he trained for three months with British commandos as an army ranger. He was wounded in action during the D-Day invasion in Normandy and died of those wounds three days later.

LINCOLN

Nelson Seaborn Drake

Birth: December 6, 1919, Wampsville, New York[459]
Death: December 19, 1944, Germany
Burial: Stockbridge Cemetery, New York

Nelson Drake graduated from Oneida High School and worked as a buffer at Oneida Limited.[460] He was working for the Keller Motor Company when he joined the army in January 1942. He married Dorothy Ano around 1943,[461] and they had a son, Gary Nelson Drake.[462] Following his training, Drake was sent to France in July 1944. He was killed in action in Europe (different reports say Belgium, Germany or France).

Donald Alton Phipps

Birth: February 5, 1924, Canastota, New York[463]
Death: August 2, 1944, Guam
Burial: Lenox Rural Cemetery, Canastota, New York

Donald Phipps graduated from Canastota High School in June 1941 and enrolled at the Hudson River State Hospital School of Nursing for one year. He worked at Oneida Limited on the assembly line of photographic trailers during the summer of 1942.[464] During that same summer, Phipps became engaged to Frances Setticase.[465] Phipps enlisted in the navy in September 1942. He trained in Newport, Rhode Island, and at Duke University, training as part of the Marines Amphibian Corps. He was sent overseas later in the fall and served at New Caledonia and Guadalcanal and took part in the invasion of Guam in a Marine Amphibian Corps. He was killed in action when he was shot while attempting to help a friend in Guam.[466] In a letter to Phipps's family following his death, Captain George F.H. Regan stated:

Image taken from the Kenwood Chronicle. *Courtesy of the Oneida Community Mansion House.*

> *I have been informed that you have been notified about Donald. He was like my next door neighbor. I live in Syracuse so I knew him very well. I assure you that he was an outstanding example of young American manhood, a good, clean and courageous lad; he was always one of the first to volunteer for any duty, regardless of how hazardous.*
>
> *On his last mission, he again volunteered for a patrol to rout out some Nips, holed up in a cave. He was one of the first to the objective, he was hit by a sniper. Your son went out as he had lived fighting for this country.*[467]

Phipps's remains were returned in 1948.[468]

MADISON

Eugene Francis Clair

Birth: May 25, 1921, Iowa[469]
Death: June 9, 1944, Bronx, New York
Burial: St. Joseph's Cemetery, Oriskany Falls, New York

At a young age, Eugene Clair and his family moved to the Solsville area, where he grew up. Following his graduation, he worked as a laborer at the local feed store.[470] He enlisted in the army in December 1940.[471] He was assigned to the Headquarters Company of the 18th Infantry and was sent to England in July 1942. He was then sent to land with the invasion forces in North Africa in November 1942. During the invasion, he was wounded and returned to the States, where he was treated at Walter Reed Hospital in Washington, D.C.[472] Clair was healthy enough to be released from the hospital, and he returned home to Solsville. Almost a year later, he entered the Veterans Hospital in the Bronx, New York, where he died in June 1944.

JOHN B. MCMULLIN

Birth: April 23, 1924, Deansboro, New York[473]
Death: February 24, 1944, Austria[474]
Burial: Cortland Rural Cemetery, New York

John McMullin attended Madison Central Schools, graduating in 1941. Prior to the war, he was working at the Nelson Creamery Corporation in Nelson. He enlisted in the U.S. Army Air Corps in November 1942. He trained in Miami Beach, Florida; Lowry Field in Colorado; Kingman, Arizona; and Dysersburg, Tennessee. Following training, he was sent to the European Theater in October 1943. He served as a side gunner in the 15th Air Force. He served in the Italian and North African Campaigns.[475] McMullin flew twenty-five missions as an armorer and gunner on a B-17. He died on a mission over Steyr, Austria. He was awarded the Air Medal with four Oak Leaf Clusters, two Purple Hearts and the Certificate of Honor. His remains were returned home in October 1948.

NELSON

CHARLES F. BLANKE

Birth: August 9, 1920, Missouri[476]
Death: January 16, 1945, Nelson, New York
Burial: Resurrection Cemetery, Afton, Missouri

Charles Blanke enrolled in the U.S. Army Air Corps in March 1943 and was trained in Santa Ana, California, before going overseas. He flew more than fifty missions as a bombardier in the European Campaign, mostly in Italy, before returning to the States around 1945.[477] While overseas, he earned an Air Medal and four Oak Leaf Clusters. Following his return to the States, he was assigned to Hendricks Field in Florida. On January 16, 1945, he was flying a training mission from Florida to Orange County, New York.[478] During the flight, there was a blinding snowstorm, and the field could not be shoveled. The plane ran out of fuel over Madison County in the town of Nelson, and eight of the ten crew abandoned ship. Blanke was the first one out, and he struck a hill before his parachute had time to deploy. He died on impact.

Robert E. Schantz

Birth: May 12, 1921, Lowville, New York[479]
Death: October 8, 1942, Guadalcanal[480]
Burial: Manila American Cemetery and Memorial, Philippines

Robert Schantz's father died in 1932. His mother remarried, and they were living in Nelson prior to the war.[481] He joined the U.S. Marines Corps in January 1942.[482] He was listed as wounded in action (shrapnel wound on his left thigh) on September 26, 1942, but returned to duty according to one account. (There was confusion over whether he returned or had died.) He was killed in action during the Battle of Guadalcanal.[483] He was posthumously awarded the Purple Heart.

ONEIDA

Raymond V. Allen

Birth: August 24, 1924, Oneida, New York[484]
Death: November 9, 1944, North Sea[485]
Burial: Lost at Sea; Memorialized at the Cambridge American Cemetery and Memorial, England

Raymond Allen graduated from Sherrill High School and went to work at Oneida Community Limited in the elevator department. He enlisted in the U.S. Army Air Corps in March 1943 at Camp Upton in New York. He trained as a radio operator at Scott Field in Illinois and then took gunnery training at Tyndall Field in Florida, where he also received his wings. He was assigned to the bomber *Bold Adventure*, which was part of the heavy bombardment group in England. He was awarded the Air Medal with three Oak Leaf Clusters for his time overseas. The award citation stated:

> *For exceptionally meritorious achievement in combat missions over enemy occupied Continental Europe.*

Image taken from the Kenwood Chronicle. *Courtesy of the Oneida Community Mansion House.*

He had completed twenty-seven missions, which included more than 250 combat hours to his credit, including 14 hours on D-Day.[486] He was lost when his plane crashed returning from a flight over Germany.[487] The plane ran into inclement weather over the North Sea. Allen bailed out over the sea, but his remains were never found.

Joseph A. Baldanza

Birth: January 20, 1916, Oneida, New York[488]
Death: January 26, 1944, North Africa[489]
Burial: St. Patrick's Cemetery, Oneida, New York

Joseph Baldanza attended and graduated from Oneida Schools before earning a degree from Rider College in Trenton, New Jersey. Following his graduation, he worked as the secretary of the Auburn State Prison Parole Board and later as a secretary at the Carrier Corporation. He enrolled in the U.S. Army Air Corps in September 1941. Baldanza's five brothers—Basil, Benjamin Jr., Frank, Louis and Victor—served in the navy during the war. Following training at Randolph Field in Texas and additional training in Oklahoma, Baldanza was sent to the Pacific, where he flew more than fifty combat missions, which entailed more than three hundred hours of flight time in the India-China combat area. He was awarded the Air Medal and Oak Leaf Cluster, the Distinguished Flying Cross and the Asiatic Ribbon. He was killed in an airplane crash in North Africa. His remains were brought home in the spring of 1948.[490]

Paul Gocht Ballard

Birth: February 27, 1919, New Britain, Connecticut[491]
Death: February 17, 1945, Germany
Burial: Lorraine American Cemetery and Memorial, France

Paul Ballard was working in New York City when he met Margaret Burnham of Oneida.[492] They got married on July 11, 1940. They had a daughter, Diana. Ballard was working at LaGuardia Field when he enlisted in the U.S. Army Air Corps in 1941. He trained as a bombardier and was sent overseas in July 1944. He was reported missing in action on February 17, 1945, after his plane failed to return from a mission over Frankfurt, Germany. He was formally declared dead one year later. He was posthumously awarded an Air Medal with four Oak Leaf Clusters, as well as a Purple Heart.

GEORGE L. BELLINGER

Birth: May 26, 1910, Fenner[493]
Death: November 26, 1945, Marshall Islands
Burial: Unknown; Memorialized at the Courts of the Missing in Honolulu Memorial, Hawaii

George Bellinger graduated from Oneida High School and was admitted to the Naval Academy, graduating in June 1932.[494] Bellinger trained as a pilot, earning a commission as a lieutenant. He married Lois Robinson in Long Beach, California, during the summer of 1932.[495] They had two sons: John, who was born in New York around 1935, and Richard, who was born in California around 1939.[496] Bellinger was assigned to a base in Pensacola, Florida, before being assigned to the Pacific Theater. He was declared missing in action in February 1942 after he did not return from an attack on the Marshall Islands. Bellinger was officially declared dead on November 26, 1945; his remains were not recovered.

MICHAEL BRUNO

Birth: February 10, 1923, Oneida, New York[497]
Death: September 24, 1945, Batavia, New York
Burial: Glenwood Cemetery, Oneida, New York

Michael Bruno graduated from Oneida School in 1942 and worked at the Oneida Casket Company before joining the army in January 1943. He joined the Quartermasters Corps, training at Camp Forrest in Tennessee, Camp Sutton in South Carolina and Fort Bragg in North Carolina before serving in England and France for eighteen months. He obtained the rank of corporal. While in France, he took ill with double pneumonia and pleurisy.[498] He spent six months in hospitals in France and England before being flown home to Utica (Rhoads Hospital) in May 1945. He was discharged from that hospital shortly after he arrived. He entered the Veterans Hospital at Batavia in August 1945 and died there.

Robert D. Buscher

Birth: September 3, 1925, Rome, New York[499]
Death: July 31, 1945, Guam
Burial: Memorials at Manila American Cemetery and Memorial, Philippines and Glenwood Cemetery, Oneida, New York

Robert Buscher grew up in Oneida and worked at the Rome airfield prior to the war. Buscher joined the navy in June 1943; he trained as a radioman on a plane and obtained the rank of seaman first class. He trained in Memphis, Tennessee; Pensacola, Florida; and San Diego, California, before he was sent to the Pacific.[500] He was killed on July 31, 1945, when the plane he was on went missing. The plane likely crashed over Guam; his remains were not recovered. He was posthumously awarded the Distinguished Flying Cross for extraordinary achievement against the Japanese from February 18 to May 24, 1945:[501]

> [F]*or extraordinary achievement while participating in aerial flight in the vicinity of China from 18 February 1945 to 24 May 1945. Seaman First Class Buscher completed twenty flights in a combat area where enemy anti-aircraft was expected to be effective or where enemy aircraft patrols usually occurred. His conduct throughout has distinguished him among those performing the duties of the same character.*

William J. Carinci

Birth: April 9, 1919, Rome, New York[502]
Death: August 12, 1944, France[503]
Burial: St. Patrick's Cemetery, Oneida, New York; Memorialized Brittany American Cemetery and Memorial, Normandy, France

William Carinci graduated from Oneida High School. Following graduation, he worked as a laborer at the Company of Master Craftsmen in Oneida.[504] He joined the New York National Guard in January 1941 before joining the U.S. Army in February 1942.[505] Carinci trained at Camp Croft in South Carolina and Camp Gordon in Georgia. He took part in the invasion of Normandy and was seriously injured on June 10, 1944.[506] He spent roughly two months at a base hospital in England.[507] He was killed in action in

August 1944 (the dates from sources state August 6, August 9 and August 12) near Mortain, France. For the events that took place on the day of his death, Carinci was posthumously awarded the Silver Star in August 1945.[508] The citation reads:

Image taken from the Kenwood Chronicle. *Courtesy of the Oneida Community Mansion House.*

> *Private 1st Class Carinci took command of his platoon after the loss of all officers in previous attempts to seize fiercely defended ground near Mortain. He quickly assembled his men and deployed them for another assault. Encountering heavy machine gun fire, Pfc. Carinci moved forward to locate the enemy emplacements. Scanning the terrain ahead, he determined that by using great care he could reach a position within 25 yards of an enemy machine gun. Crawling forward, inch by inch, with utter disregard for his own personal safety he finally reached the selected point without detection.*
>
> *Suddenly rising up, he hurled a grenade with such accuracy that the enemy gun and its crew were destroyed. Again leading his men forward, this time with fixed bayonets, Pfc. Carinci closed with the enemy and took their position. During the assault Pfc. Carinci was hit and made the supreme sacrifice. Pfc. Carinci's heroic and fearless devotion to duty reflect great credit upon himself and the military service.*

William's brother Sergeant James Carinci was wounded in February 1944 on Eniwetok Island and in June of the same year on Saipan, and his brother Joseph survived the sinking of the USS *Plymouth* off the coast of South Carolina on August 5, 1943.

DONALD J. CUNNINGHAM

Birth: February 23, 1921, Syracuse, New York[509]
Death: December 9, 1943
Burial: Lost at Sea; Memorial Glenwood Cemetery, Oneida, New York

Donald Cunningham graduated from Oneida High School in 1939 and enrolled at the Admiral Farragut Academy in Pine Beach, New Jersey, graduating in 1940. Following his graduation, he worked as a linesman for the New York Power & Light Corporation until he enlisted in the U.S. Army Air Corps in March 1942. He trained at Maxwell Field, Alabama; Selmen Field, Monroe, Louisiana; and Navigators School at Coral Cables, Florida. Cunningham was commissioned a second lieutenant in March 1943 and trained as a navigator. In April 1943, he married Miss Rita Jane Carson of Oneida in St. Joseph, Missouri, while he was stationed at Rosecrans Airfield. He was assigned to Nashville, where he made several trips to South America, Europe and Asia. On December 8, 1943, the flight he was on was lost somewhere in the Atlantic. The army sent the family the following account a year later:

> *Since Second Lieutenant Donald J. Cunningham, 080640, Air Corps was reported missing 9 December 1943 the War Department has entertained the hope that he survived and that information would be revealed dispelling the uncertainty surrounding his absence. However, as in many cases, the conditions of warfare deny us such information. The record concerning your son and husband shows that on December 9, 1943, he departed from Goose Bay, Labrador on a Flying Fortress, which failed to reach its destination in the United Kingdom. The last message from the crew was an SOS giving their position as four hundred fifty miles south of Iceland. Rescue planes were dispatched and searched an area of approximately two hundred square miles without finding a trace of the crew or their plane.*
>
> *The remainder of the letter set forth that according to provisions of Public Law 490, an official finding of death has been recorded and concluded: "I regret the necessity for this message but trust that the ending of a long period of uncertainty may give at least some small measure of consolation. I hope you may find sustaining comfort in the thought that the uncertainty with which war has surrounded the absence of Lieutenant Cunningham has enhanced the honor of his service to his country and of his sacrifice."*[510]

Courtesy of Eileen Kinsella.

Cunningham's remains were not recovered. Donald's father, Leonard, was an ambulance driver in World War I who served sixteen months in France. During the early part of World War II, Leonard served as a sub-district director of the Aircraft Warning Service of Madison County. Following his son's enlistment, Leonard joined the

Construction Battalion of the navy as a petty officer second class. Leonard owned two businesses in Oneida: the Glenwood Dairy and the Explosive Supply Company Inc. Leonard's wife, Anna, operated his two businesses while he was serving.

ORION (ORIN) E. DUNSTER

Birth: March 25, 1918, Morristown, New York[511]
Death: November 13, 1944, France
Burial: Lakeside Rural Cemetery, Bernhards Bay, New York

Orion Dunster married Eva Pierce, and they had a son, Orion E. Dunster Jr. He worked at Oneida Limited in the carbine slide department prior to entering the service in December 1943. He was wounded in action in July 1944 and received the Purple Heart. He returned to action and was killed in action. For his actions, Dunster was posthumously awarded the Bronze Star.[512] The citation (which was partially redacted) reads as follows:

> [O]*n 13 November 1944. During the operations against *** the platoon leader of the Third Platoon, Company G, *** Infantry, became a casualty. Sergeant Dunster, a platoon sergeant, immediately assumed command of the platoon and advancing at the head of his men, successfully entered the village. Stubborn enemy resistance, marked by intense sniper fire, made it necessary that the platoon have adequate cover at once. As Sergeant Dunster made his way across a street in order to give protecting fire to his platoon while it sought cover, he was killed by enemy fire. Sergeant Dunster's leadership, courage and devotion to duty reflect credit upon his character as a soldier.*

Dunster's remains were returned in 1949.

ALEXANDER B. DURKEE

Birth: February 25, 1922, Oneida, New York[513]
Death: January 15, 1945
Burial: West Verona Cemetery, Verona, New York

Alexander Durkee graduated from Oneida High School and worked as a machinist for the Westcott Chuck Company prior to entering the service in March 1943.[514] He trained as a P-51 Mustang pilot and fought in the European Theater. He completed more than twenty-five missions in support of ground operations and was part of the pioneer P-51 Mustang fighter group of the 19th Tactical Air Command, which was awarded the Presidential Unit Citation. In November 1944, he was awarded the Air Medal and two Oak Leaf Clusters for meritorious achievement. In January 1945, Durkee was declared missing in action in after a mission in the Ardennes, northeast of Bastogne, Germany.[515] Durkee received a Silver Star for his actions that day. The citation reads in part:

> *Durkee was leading his squadron on an attack against important enemy armored forces and command posts in the Ardennes, northeast of Bastogne. He demonstrated outstanding courage and brilliant leadership on this occasion. Although his plane sustained severe anti-aircraft damage, Durkee without regard for his personal safety, retained leadership of his flight and pressed home his attacks, destroying a vast amount of armored vehicles, enemy command posts and other vital equipment.*

Durkee was declared killed in action in Luxemburg on January 16, 1945.[516] His remains were returned home in April 1949, and he is buried at the West Verona Cemetery.

Donald Dwight Earl

Birth: August 14, 1918, Utica, New York[517]
Death: May 4, 1945, Okinawa, Japan
Burial: Mount Pleasant Cemetery, Canastota, New York

Donald Earl attended Fayetteville High School and was working at a garage in Canastota when he enlisted in the marines in January 1942. He trained at Parris Island in South Carolina and Anacostia in Washington, D.C. In October 1942, he was sent to New Guinea and assigned to the 1st Marine Division. He was wounded in action on Palau on September 17, 1944. He was awarded the Purple Heart for this action. He was killed in action during the Battle of Okinawa. Earl's remains were returned in January 1949.[518]

WILBER NOYES EARL

Birth: November 28, 1914, Oneida, New York[519]
Death: October 1, 1944, France
Burial: Lorraine American Cemetery and Memorial, France; Memorial, Oneida Community Cemetery, New York

Courtesy of Polly Held

Wilber Earl graduated from Sherrill High School and enrolled at Amherst College, graduating from Amherst in 1936.[520] Following graduation, he was working as a salesman for the William A. Rogers Division of Oneida Limited. He enlisted in the army in March 1941. He trained at the infantry school and later Officers Training School in Fort Benning, Georgia, and upon graduation, he was commissioned a second lieutenant. Following graduation, he married Charlotte Welch of Chicago. They had one son, Wilber Noyes Earl Jr., in 1943. In June 1943, he was promoted to captain. Earl served as a commander of a rifle company with the 79th division of the 3rd Army. He continued training in Kansas before going overseas in April 1944. He arrived in France on June 11. He was killed in action in France and was posthumously awarded the Silver Star.[521] The citation reads:

> [O]*n 1 October 1944 in France. In the Foret de Parroy under intense enemy artillery and mortar fire, Captain Earl displayed exemplary leadership in directing his company attack. Disregarding his own safety, he repeatedly moved to the front of his attacking platoons to reorganize and personally lead them forward two thousand yards to achieve the battalion objective. The courageous leadership and outstanding devotion to duty exhibited by Captain Earl reflect highest credit on himself and the armed forces of the United States.*

Franklin R. Gowing

Birth: November 10, 1922, Manatee, Florida[522]
Death: August 2, 1944, France
Burial: Normandy American Cemetery and Memorial, France; Memorial, Lakeside Cemetery, Sackets Harbor, New York

Franklin Gowing attended grade school in Florida before moving to Oneida, graduating from Oneida High School in 1942. Following graduation, he worked at Revere Copper and Brass in Rome, New York, before enlisting in the U.S. Army Air Corps in January 1943. He trained as a pilot of the P-51 Mustang fighter in San Antonio, Texas, before heading overseas in May 1944. On August 2, 1944, his plane was struck by flack while flying over Saint-Pois, France, while escorting bombers on a mission, and he was listed as missing. In January 1945, he was reported dead.

Donald C. Harrington

Birth: January 2, 1921, Kendall, New York[523]
Death: March 29, 1943, Tunisia
Burial: St. Helena's Cemetery, Oneida, New York

Donald Harrington graduated from Oneida High School in 1938 and took postgraduate classes in civics and chemistry. He enlisted in the army in January 1941 and trained as a surgical technician in the Medical Corps. He trained in Plattsburgh, New York; Fort Devens in Massachusetts; Camp Blanding in Florida; Fort Benning in Georgia; and Indiantown, Pennsylvania. Harrington was sent overseas in 1942 and served in England and Scotland before going into North Africa in November 1942. In December 1942, he wrote a letter to his family about his disgust over strikes taking place in the United States:

Image taken from the Kenwood Chronicle. *Courtesy of the Oneida Community Mansion House.*

> *Every person who strikes at a time like this should be immediately inducted and sent out here with us—or to one of the other bitter fronts which are being held by their former friends.*[524]

He was killed in action in Tunisia. Harrington was posthumously awarded the Silver Star.[525] The citation states:

> [F]*or gallantry in action while engaged in military operations involving conflict with an armed hostile force while serving with the Medical Detachment, 26th Infantry Regiment, 1st Infantry Division, in action against the enemy in the vicinity of Gafsa, Tunisia, on 29 March 1943. His gallant actions and dedicated devotion to duty, without regard for his own life, were in keeping with the highest traditions of military service and reflect great credit upon himself, his unit and the United States Army.*[526]

Harrington's remains returned home in 1948.[527]

Raymond F. Harsma

Birth: April 16, 1920, Oneida, New York[528]
Death: July 4, 1944[529]
Burial: Lost at Sea; Memorialized at St. Helena's Cemetery, Oneida, New York; Courts of the Missing, Honolulu Memorial

Raymond Harsma graduated from Oneida High School and enrolled in Niagara University. Upon graduation from Niagara in 1943, Harsma entered the navy and was assigned to Navy Officers' School at Notre Dame University. Upon graduation from Officer's School, he was commissioned an ensign and was then assigned to Submarines School in New London, Connecticut.[530] He married Jean Samal on February 19, 1944, in Albany.[531] He was assigned to the South Pacific and eventually was placed on the submarine USS *S-28*. The USS *S-28* was lost at sea during drills off the coast of Hawaii. The submarine lost contact at 6:20 p.m. and was never heard from beyond a diesel fuel slick from near where it was lost two days later. Harmsa was among the forty-nine men who died on the sub; all their remains were lost at sea.

Earlis (Carlis) V. Hasty

Birth: September 8, 1911, Sioux City, Iowa[532]
Death: September 21, 1944, Oneida, New York
Burial: McConnellsville Cemetery, McConnellsville, New York

Earlis Hasty moved with his mother and siblings to Oneida after 1920. Prior to the war, he worked at Oneida Limited and a local diner. He was drafted into the army in July 1942. In September 1944, Hasty returned home on a furlough from Camp Foster in Texas. After borrowing a .22-caliber rifle, he went hunting. He did not return home at an expected time, and a search party was formed. The following morning, Hasty was found by his stepfather, William Bybee, with a self-inflicted gunshot wound.

Robert L. Hollis

Birth: August 18, 1921, Oneida, New York[533]
Death: September 24, 1945, Alder Creek, New York[534]
Burial: St. Francis Cemetery, Durhamville, New York

Robert Hollis grew up in Oneida and attended local schools. Prior to the war, he was working at Montgomery Ward in Rome. He enlisted in the Marine Corps in June 1942. He trained at a clerical school in Philadelphia, Pennsylvania, and Quantico, Virginia, before being selected for the V-5 training course.[535] He trained at the Pre-Flight School in Chapel Hill, North Carolina, and followed that up with advanced training in Bunker Hill, Indiana. He continued his training in Pensacola, where he received his commission as a second lieutenant in March 1945.[536] After receiving his commission, he married Jean R. Rankin on March 24, 1945.[537] Hollis planned a surprise visit for his parents' thirty-second anniversary in September 1945.[538] He took off in a Corsair plane from Cherry Point, North Carolina, and was flying to Rome Air Field. While flying over the Catskills, he radioed that he was having engine trouble. Hollis was last heard from on September 24, 1945, at 1:45 p.m. Hollis was missing for more than a year before his remains were discovered in the Alder Creek area of the Adirondacks by hunters on October 27, 1946. Following his death, Jean gave birth to a daughter in December 1945.

Robert Merriman Howd

Birth: July 10, 1920, Utica, New York[539]
Death: July 2, 1944, Yugoslavia[540]
Burial: Memorial at Tablet of the Missing at the Florence American Cemetery and Memorial, Toscana, Italy

Robert Howd grew up in Oneida, graduating from Oneida Junior High School and attending one year of high school in Oneida before his family moved to New Hartford. He graduated in 1939. Following his graduation, he worked at the Savage Arms Corporation in Utica before enlisting in the National Guard in October 1940. He trained at Camp McClennan in Alabama and was assigned to the Army Postal Service before he was assigned to active duty in December 1941. He transferred to the air corps in late 1942 and started his training in January 1943. Howd trained in Santa Ana, Ontario and Gardner Field, California, before being commissioned a lieutenant in November 1943 in Yuma, Arizona. He continued training in Salt Lake City, Utah; Alexandria, Louisiana; and Langley Field, Virginia, before going to North Africa, where he served as a copilot in a B-17 Flying Fortress. He flew several bombing missions over Italy. He was killed in action when the plane he was in crashed somewhere over Yugoslavia.

Stewart A. Jones

Birth: December 19, 1920, North Tonawanda, New York[541]
Death: May 8, 1944, Corregidor
Burial: Manila American Cemetery and Memorial, Philippines.

Stewart Jones graduated from Oneida High School in 1939, served briefly in the Civilian Conservation Corps and then entered the army shortly thereafter.[542] He trained at Fort McDowell before going overseas.[543] He was declared missing in May 1942 while serving at Corregidor. In May 1944, he was declared dead. Brigadier General Robert H. Dunlop wrote the family:

> *The finding does not establish any true or probable date of death; however as required by law, it includes a presumptive date of death for termination*

> *of pay and allowance, settlement of accounts and payment of death gratuities. In the case of your son this date has been set as May 8, 1944.*
>
> *I regret the necessity for this message but trust that the ending of a long period of uncertainty may give at least some measure of consolation. An appraisal of the suffering endured and the sacrifices made by your son in the service of his country compels in us feelings of humility and respect. May Providence grant a measure of relief from the anguish and anxiety you may have experienced during these many months.*[544]

In August 1945, notices say that he died from "dysentery, starvation and malnutrition" while he was a prisoner in a Japanese prison camp. His remains were discovered in 1947.[545]

JAMES VINCENT LATTERI

Birth: June 6, 1913, Oneida, New York[546]
Death: July 2, 1943, Rochester, New York[547]
Burial: St. Patrick's Cemetery, Oneida, New York

James Latteri grew up in Oneida and graduated from local schools. He married Frances M. Roder on January 8, 1939.[548] They had a son, James V. Latteri, in 1941.[549] He worked as a mechanic at different auto stations in Oneida and Sherrill prior to enlisting.[550] He enlisted in the navy in November 1942. He trained at Sampson Naval Training Station in New York. He achieved the rank of motor machinist second class.[551] He was killed in a car accident in Rochester, New York, one week before he was scheduled to graduate.

DONALD L. MACARTHUR

Birth: March 28, 1920, Wampsville, New York[552]
Death: January 2, 1944, South Pacific[553]
Burial: Memorialized at the Columns of the Missing, National Memorial of the Pacific, Hawaii

Donald MacArthur spent part of his youth living in Oneida before moving to Rochester, New York, and later to Alhambra, California. He graduated from Alhambra High School before enrolling at Pasadena Junior College and later the University of California–Los Angeles before joining the U.S. Army Air Corps in 1942. He married his wife, Shirley, but does not appear to have had children. Upon completing his training, he was shipped to the Pacific and earned a Bronze Oak Leaf Cluster for his parts in raids on Nauru and Tarawa. He was promoted to captain. While on leave with his wife, MacArthur spoke about his experiences overseas:

> *Our Squadron went down to the South Pacific en masse and we operated from a small island. It was one of those South Sea Isles you read about—sandy beaches, palm trees and natives still living by the old customs.*
>
> *We raided the Japs twice. Once we raided one of their bases on the Island of Nauru. When we were dropping our bombs on them it really seemed hard for me to realize that we were dropping real bombs on people. It was hard to realize that the black puffs of smoke that were breaking all around us were real flak and that they make nasty little holes in planes.*
>
> *We encountered some Jap aircraft resistance but they seemed very reluctant to come in close, so we didn't get many good shots at them. My top turret man was quite sure that he hit one. One of the Nips got a good burst into one of our planes with his 20-millimeter guns and did some damage to Jake's rudder. Jake is the guy that was flying the ship and he did a marvelous job of it too.*
>
> *Another of our boys got some lead. A 20-millimeter went through the radio man's window and hit the top turret man in the foot. With his toes blown away the man stayed with his guns and hit a Jap. Another 20-millimeter shell went into the rear of his ship and caused quite a bit of damage. It wounded some men and one of them died later. All of our ships got back OK and we did a hell of a lot of damage to Tojo. More in fact than I realized myself. We all took pictures of the target and I saw those pictures the other day. I don't think the Nips will forget that raid for quite a while.*
>
> *Our first raid was carried off on the 20th and two nights later on the 22nd, the Japs paid us a visit. It was about three in the morning when Jack Drenan woke me up with "Hey Mac, it's an air raid."*
>
> *It was kind of hard to believe but when I got outside the tent everyone was running to fox holes and I could hear the planes over us. We all ran to the nearest fox holes. The holes are about five feet across and three feet deep. The Japs didn't bomb right away because of cloud coverage and we*

all huddled together in the holes, wondered if it was true and what the first bomb would sound like.

We soon found out.

When the clouds opened up the Nips laid their eggs. God, what a sound! I'll never forget it. I don't think any of us will. The bombs sound like sky rockets, when they're falling then they go "Karumph" when they hit. Those that were close—40 feet away showered sparks and red hot shrapnel. Some of the boys, who were still running for holes when the bombs hit, got it badly. I saw one of them lying beside a road next morning. He looked just like he had laid down on his side to sleep. There were two more under a truck that had been buried about 25 feet. They were a terrible, unbelievable sight. I just can't tell you. The same bomb got them all.

I had the pleasure of going on another raid after that when we bombed them on the island of Tarawa. We bombed them at night. We lost our formation about three-fourths of the way so we had to go in alone. Ted did some marvelous navigation. When we got there we flew some evasive action over the target and I cut the motors several times just to worry them as they did us. We made a good run and got rid of all our bombs. I'm sure we did a lot of damage. They fired ack-ack at us but we didn't get hit. That tracer didn't look so good coming at us, though. I was really glad to get out of there.

Don't think for a minute that I wasn't scared. I've never been more terrified all my life. There's not one man who was there who won't admit the same thing. It's not so bad when you're in the air because then you have a fighting chance but when you're on the ground in a hole, just waiting, it's hell. You can hear the bombs falling right down the line and come closer. It's really no fun.

Well, we're back in the Hawaiian Islands now and all my crew is OK. I don't know when we're going back.

By the way if you ever have any air raid drill, take it seriously, for God's sake, and try to tell everyone else to. I don't want you to ever go through that hell. That's why we have to end this damned war soon.[554]

MacArthur's plane was shot down on January 2, 1944; his remains were not recovered.[555]

Richard C. Perling

Birth: October 4, 1921, Oneida, New York[556]
Death: August 9, 1942, Solomon Islands
Burial: Remains Not Recovered; Memorialized, Tablet of the Missing, Manila American Cemetery and Memorial & Glenwood Cemetery, Oneida, New York

Richard Perling graduated from Oneida High School in 1939. He enlisted in the navy in April 1940 and was trained as a radioman. Following the completion of his training, he was assigned to the USS *Vincennes* in the Pacific Fleet.[557] He was killed in action when the ship was sunk near the Solomon Islands. Perling's remains were never recovered. According to a telegram the family received:

> *The Navy Department deeply regrets to inform you that your son, Richard Charles Perling, radioman, third class, US Navy was killed in action in the performance of his duty and in the service of his country. The Department extends to you its sincerest sympathy in your great loss....* [C]*onditions made impossible the recovery of the body and cautioned the parents against disclosing the name of the vessel on which their son was serving, because of its value to the enemy.*

Arthur C. Pflanz

Birth: December 15, 1915, Utica, New York[558]
Death: December 2, 1944, Germany
Burial: Crown Hill Memorial Park, Clinton, New York

Arthur Pflanz attended school in Utica and Vernon. Upon graduation, he worked for the John F. Wallin Coal Company in Oneida as a truck driver.[559] He married Gladys Kinne of Rome in January 1935.[560] He enlisted in the army in September 1943.[561] He trained at Camp Blanding in Florida and Fort George Meade in Maryland before being assigned to the 121st Infantry and going overseas in July 1944.[562] He fought in battles in France and Luxembourg. Pflanz was reported missing in action in Germany in December 1944. In March 1945, he was reported as killed in action in Germany.

Arlington C. Raymond

Birth: July 9, 1918, State Bridge, New York[563]
Death: April 3, 1945, Germany[564]
Burial: Lorraine American Cemetery and Memorial, France

Arlington Raymond married Betty Cullen on January 14, 1939.[565] They had two daughters, Karen and Marguerite.[566] Prior to the war, he worked as a trucker and at Oneida Limited as a buffer.[567] He enlisted in the army in April 1944. He served as an ammunition truck driver in Germany.[568] He was killed in action in Wurzburg, Germany. Raymond was posthumously awarded a Silver Star. The citation partially states:

> *The President of the United States of America, authorized by Act of Congress July 9, 1918, takes pride in presenting the Silver Star (posthumously) to Private Arlington C. Raymond, for gallantry in action while serving with Company A, 142d Engineer Combat Battalion, 42d Infantry Division, in action on 3 April 1945 at Wurzburg, Germany. As a member of an assault boat crew, Private Raymond participated in numerous crossings of the Main River in the face of intense artillery, machine gun, and small arms fire. On his final return trip, due to the casualties among crewmembers, he loaded his boat with prisoners and ordered them to paddle back. Midway in the stream, machine gun fire struck some of the prisoners and demoralized the others to such an extent that control of the boat was lost and it started to drift into enemy territory. In an attempt to save the boat so vital to the mission, Private Raymond leaped into the water, attempting to swim and push the boat to the friendly shore. Though fatigued and weary and under intense fire, he labored to propel the boat until exhaustion overcame him and he disappeared from sight. Private Raymond's great courage and heroic gallantry were instrumental in establishing the bridgehead and instilled in his comrades the determination that contributed to the eventual capture of Wurzburg.*[569]

Jonah Reeves

Birth: August 22, 1922, Oneida, New York[570]
Death: July 4, 1943, Germany[571]
Burial: Remains Not Recovered; Memorialized at Runnymede Memorial, England

Jonah Reeves grew up in Oneida and Durhamville before graduating from Oneida High School in 1940. Following graduation, he enrolled in Hamilton College in Clinton, studying math and pre-medicine.[572] While there, he was one of ten students who enrolled in the Civilian Pilot Training Course, which was offered through the college.[573] He left the school to enlist in the 9th Squadron of the Royal Canadian Air Force in Ottawa, Ontario, Canada, in November 1941. He trained as a navigator and went overseas in September 1942. He flew missions over France, Italy, Denmark, Holland, Germany and Sweden while overseas.[574] On July 4, 1943, Reeves was part of a bombing mission that crashed near Cologne, Germany, close to the borders of the Netherlands and Belgium. In May 1944, he was declared officially dead.

Robert Roney

Birth: July 21, 1911, Oneida, New York[575]
Death: October 16, 1943, Texas
Burial: St. Mary's Irish Ridge Cemetery, Verona, New York

Robert Roney attended St. Patrick's Parochial School. Following school, Roney worked at Oneida Limited and later as a bus driver for the Central New York Coach Lines on the Syracuse-Utica Run. He had a daughter, Elizabeth Ann Roney, who was born around 1936. Roney joined the army in December 1942. While he was assigned to the army air base at Pyote, Texas, he was accidentally shot and killed by a civilian.[576]

Joseph C. Rule

Birth: September 18, 1916, Ottawa, Ontario, Canada[577]
Death: December 14, 1944, France
Burial: Henry-Chapelle American Cemetery and Memorial, Belgium

Joseph Rule graduated from Pulaski Academy and then moved to Oneida, where he worked as a chef at Webster's Diner.[578] He married Fannie Panzica of Oneida on October 4, 1941. Rule was inducted into the army in October 1943; he went overseas in July 1944 to the European Theater.[579] He was wounded and captured on August 12, 1944, but released on the same day. He was awarded the Purple Heart and the Infantry Combat Medal. Rule was killed in action in France.

Joseph Thomas Sansone

Birth: October 22, 1916, Oswego, New York[580]
Death: August 17, 1945, Died at Sea[581]
Burial: St. Paul's Cemetery, Oswego, New York

Thomas Sansone attended St. Mary's Parochial School in Oswego and, upon graduation, worked as a chef at a restaurant, the Shady Grill, owned by his uncle in Oneida. He entered the service in April 1942. He obtained the rank of sergeant and served with the 15th Army Air Force in North Africa, Sicily and Italy. He transferred to the Army Corps of Engineers, where he served out the remainder of his service. He was on a ship returning home when he died after ulcers in his stomach ruptured. Following his death, Sansone's company commander, Robert F. Potter, sent a letter to his parents:

> *You have already received through regular War Department Channels the saddening information that your son Joseph died at sea during the trip of an Army transport to the United States.*
>
> *As his company commander I should like to be among the first to express my personal condolences and those of his comrades. We are fully aware of the sorrow and grief which come with the loss of your beloved son at a time when the signs of peace are so apparent. We realize too, how feeble are words to assuage the tears in the bereavement of your family.*
>
> *It must be comforting, however, to know that Joseph gave his life freely while in the service of his country, and that sacrifices that he made in the service insure for him the undying gratitude of the nation he loved so well. While your son was in our unit but a short time, due to the transfer of troops in redeployment, yet his service record is testimony of his efficiency, loyalty and other qualities which combined to make of him a good American soldier. As a result he was a credit to his family and the uniform he worse so gallantly. In addition to his fidelity to the religion of his conviction resulted in his receiving the last rites at the hands of the Catholic Chaplain aboard ship*
>
> *Again please be assured of our heartfelt sympathy and acknowledging always the designs of Providence.*[582]

Robert H. Seifert

Birth: December 3, 1920, Oneida, New York[583]
Death: April 15, 1944, Holland[584]
Burial: Remains Not Recovered; Memorialized on Tablet of the Missing at the Cambridgeshire American Cemetery, England.

Robert Seifert graduated from Oneida High School in 1938.[585] He enrolled at the Albany State Teachers College and graduated from there with a degree in mathematics and physics on June 1, 1942. The day after his graduation, he enlisted in the U.S. Army Air Corps. He trained as a P-51 Mustang pilot in the 8th Air Force in San Antonio, Texas (Pre-Flight); Independence, Kansas (Preliminary Training); and Missouri before being commissioned a lieutenant at Mission Field in Texas in October 1943. Following his commission, he continued training at Dale Maybre Field and Bartow Field in Florida. He was sent to the European Theater around March 1944. On April 15, 1944, his plane disappeared while on a mission over Holland. In November 1945, he was declared dead.[586]

Norman R. Short

Birth: February 21, 1915, Ogdensburg, New York[587]
Death: July 28, 1943, Munda
Burial: St. Helena's Cemetery, Oneida, New York

Norman Short's family moved to Vernon around 1920, and he graduated from Vernon High School in 1932. Prior to the war, he worked at Oneida Limited in the Polishing Department.[588] He enlisted in the 106th Infantry of the Oneida National Guard.[589] He was a sergeant when the unit traveled south to camp in October 1940. He was then sent to Officers Training School in Fort Benning, Georgia. Upon his graduation, Short was commissioned a second lieutenant. He was promoted to first lieutenant after being sent overseas. He was killed in action in the Munda area of the South Pacific.[590]

Image taken from the Kenwood Chronicle. *Courtesy of the Oneida Community Mansion House.*

Thomas W. Skinner

Birth: May 4, 1916, Oneida, New York[591]
Death: March 13, 1945, Italy[592]
Burial: Oneida Castle Cemetery, Oneida Castle, New York

Thomas Skinner grew up in Oneida Castle, and after attending local schools, he worked as a millwright in a silverware factory (likely Oneida Limited).[593] He joined Company K of the 10th Infantry in the National Guard, based in Oneida in October 1940.[594] His obituaries state that he had a wife living in Dallas, Texas, but did not list a name. Skinner was reassigned to a light infantry unit and transferred overseas in January 1945. He was killed in action in Italy. His remains were returned home in May 1948.

James G. Townsend

Birth: January 31, 1924, Oneida, New York[595]
Death: June 7, 1944, France[596]
Burial: Normandy American Cemetery, France; Memorial, Oneida Community Cemetery, New York

James Townsend's father was a salesman with Oneida Limited, and the family moved to Missouri when he was young. The family moved back to Oneida around 1942. He trained as a paratrooper. Townsend was killed in action during the invasion of France. He was posthumously awarded the Purple Heart. Following his death, Townsend's family received a letter written by James shortly before he died.

> *Well tonight's the night in which will be unleashed the greatest invasion force ever known upon Europe.*
>
> *If I don't come out of this thing I want my people (especially my Father) to know I gave every ounce of my strength and energy for what I believe I am fighting for. Be it here stated that I am not entering this thing with a complete blind trust in God but what I consider equally, if not more important—faith in myself and my fellow men.*
>
> *I am going to be among the first to go in as the parachutists spearhead the attack; the infantry will come in a little later and relieve us.*
>
> *Chin up folks and carry on!*
>
> *Jim*

HARRY H. VAN AUKEN

Birth: August 19, 1918, Oneida, New York[597]
Death: February 16, 1945
Burial: Glenwood Cemetery, Oneida, New York

Harry Van Auken attended Oneida High School and enrolled in a Civilian Conservation Corps Camp before going to work at Oneida Limited in the Silver Buff Department. He married Sophie Bigda, and they had one son, Frederick James. He enlisted in the army in December 1940 and spent more than two years at Fort Lewis in Washington in the Adjutant General's Office before going overseas in August 1944. In October 1944, Van Auken was transferred to the infantry. Van Auken wrote a letter to Reay Milnes, personnel manager of Oneida Limited, on January 3, 1945:

Image taken from the Kenwood Chronicle. *Courtesy of the Oneida Community Mansion House.*

> *Shortly after my arrival overseas I transferred to the infantry in the grade of Private. My former job in the Adjutant General's Office, far behind the lines, didn't prove very interesting. I believe that Frederick James (16 months now) will be a little more proud of his Daddy as an Infantry soldier....I am in a machine gun company and am well satisfied. We have sort of a "front-seat" now, so to speak.*
>
> *I have visited Cherbourg, Normandy and saw the famous Eiffel Tower in Paris. It is permissible to state we are now part of the 7th Army in France.*
>
> *Effective December 11, I was awarded the Combat Infantryman's Badge for successful offensive action against the enemy. It entitles the soldier an additional ten dollars raise in pay, I believe I will accept it!*
>
> *Usually after we fight for a town, we are compensated by being able to obtain shelter and clean up. Like now, I'm writing to you from within a house that still has most of the roof left on it. We have a stove in the room and are comfortable. We quickly learn to appreciate what we have, so some good comes from War, if only in a small way.*
>
> *We spent a very sober New Year's Eve. However, we saw the New Year come in with a "bang" in more ways than one! We got 1945 off to a good*

start at the expense of the Krauts, so this may be our year of Victory. We will do our best to make it that.

We are encouraged by the effort that has been put forth by the folks back home in producing the materials we need over here. We are truly the finest equipped Army in the world.

Van Auken died from wounds received in action. His remains were returned in 1948.

Richard N. Van Nostrand

Birth: April 11, 1922, New York[598]
Death: November 14, 1944, Philippines[599]
Burial: Sunnyside Cemetery, Lincoln, New York

Richard Van Nostrand grew up in Oneida and joined the U.S. Army Air Corps in April 1941. He was stationed at Fort Dix in New Jersey; Savannah, Georgia; Bradley Field in Connecticut; Roosevelt Field in Long Island; Dow Field in Bangor, Maine; Syracuse Air Base; Briggs Field in Texas; New Guinea; and the Philippines. He went overseas around January 1942. He served as a crew chief, and on July 15, 1943, he received a commendation, which read:

Image taken from the Kenwood Chronicle. *Courtesy of the Oneida Community Mansion House.*

*A Combat plane **** undoubtedly saved from total destruction by the prompt and exemplary conduct of this alert crew in the face of grave personal danger.*

*On July 15, 1943 **** this airplane was approaching the strip in a southwesterly direction with smoke trailing from the left engine. Shortly before actual landing, flame burst from the engine and enveloped the entire motor.*

Staff Sergeant Van Nostrand jumped into a jeep and started for the plane, which was on the ground but still moving rapidly. The balance of the alert crew in the two alert trucks closely followed him.

Because of the urgency of the situation, these men did not even pause to don asbestos suits. As soon as the plane stopped rolling, Sergeant Van Nostrand attacked the flames with a small carbon tetrachloride extinguisher, which was in the jeep, but this was ineffectual.

Very shortly after that the two alert trucks containing the large extinguishers, arrived at the plane. All these men immediately put the extinguishers into operation and extinguished the fire.

No members of either the airplane or alert crews were injured, and the prompt action of the alert crew of the squadron with total disregard for personal safety, not only prevented possible injury to personnel but also saved from total loss a valuable combat plane which will soon be flying again.[600]

Van Nostrand was killed in action on November 14, 1944. In a letter to the family, an army chaplain wrote:

It is with deepest regret that I must write concerning the death of Staff Sergeant Van Nostrand who was killed in action while performing his duties on an airstrip somewhere in the Philippines. His death was from enemy action over the strip.

Richard was an able crew chief and well liked by men in his squadron. The fortunes of war dictate that some men are bound to lose their lives. He was one of many who have in this world struggle. But you may be sure Richard gave his life nobly in the service of his country. Many men live long lives, but without nobility, and that is no particular credit to them. But of those who live nobly, and who serve the cause of mankind well, it can be said that they are truly great and that the imprint of their service will never be blotted out.

Appropriate services have been held and he has been placed in the cemetery here. We all deeply mourn his untimely death and extend our heartfelt sympathy to your sorrow.[601]

Louis H. Veling

Birth: February 5, 1915, Oneida, New York[602]
Death: March 18, 1944
Burial: Common Grave at Zachary Taylor National Cemetery, Louisville, Kentucky; Memorial, St. Francis Cemetery, Durhamville, New York

Louis Veling graduated from Oneida High School. Prior to enlisting in the service, Veling worked at Oneida Limited in the plating department.[603]

Image taken from the Kenwood Chronicle. *Courtesy of the Oneida Community Mansion House.*

He joined Company K of the 106th Infantry Unit of the New York National Guard in October 1940, serving one year in Newfoundland before transferring to the U.S. Army Air Corps. He completed his training in July 1943, and he was commissioned a second lieutenant in Eagle Pass, Texas. He married Delma Blanken from Oklahoma on July 31, 1943. In December 1943, he transferred to the transport service in India. Veling was a transport pilot in Asia flying the dangerous route over the Himalayan Mountains. He was killed in action when the plane he was piloting crashed. A letter from General George Marshall stated that Veling had

> *been piloting troop carrying planes as well as supplies over hazardous routes.*

He was posthumously awarded a Purple Heart Medal and an Air Medal award with an Oak Leaf Cluster. The citation for the Air Medal reads:

> [F]*or meritorious achievement while participating, as pilot, between 1 January 1944 and 18 March 1944 in operational flights totaling more than 100 hours in unarmed, heavily loaded transport airplanes, during which exposure to enemy fire was probable and expected.*
>
> *During the periods indicated, he has completed flights from bases in Upper Assam, providing food, clothing, mail, medicinal supplies, and material to our forward elements and to those of our Indian, British and Chiles Allies in the hills and mountains of Upper Burma.*
>
> *Undaunted by the hazards faced regularly and continuously, Lieutenant Veling performed his duties in such a manner that the highest credit is reflected upon himself and the military forces of the United States.*[604]

Veling's remains were returned in January 1950.

Charles B. Watkins

Birth: January 30, 1915, Ilion, New York[605]
Death: July 27, 1945, Northern Luzon[606]
Burial: Manila American Cemetery, Philippines

Charles Watkins's family moved around before settling in Oneida. Prior to the war, he worked as a mill hand at the National Casket Company in Oneida.[607] He married Leita Mae McCumber in November 1942. They had one son, Charles, who was born in November 1944 but who died shortly afterward.[608] Watkins joined the National Guard in March 1937; he was discharged in November 1938 and rejoined in October 1940. He transferred to the army in 1941 and trained at the Chemical Warfare School.[609] His training included decontamination treatment of gas casualties and chemical warfare material and tactics. Upon completion of the training, he served as his unit's gas officer and chemical warfare instructor. He was commissioned a second lieutenant. He was killed in action in Northern Luzon.

SMITHFIELD

LaVerne Alfred Austin

Birth: July 25, 1923, Fenner, New York[610]
Death: December 7, 1941, Pearl Harbor, Hawaii
Burial: Peterboro Cemetery, Peterboro, New York

LaVerne Austin enlisted in the navy while a senior at Cazenovia Central School on December 7, 1940. He initially was trained in Newport, Rhode Island, before transferring to San Diego, California, and later Pearl Harbor, Hawaii, in August 1941; he was assigned to the USS *Arizona*. He achieved the rank of seaman second class. Austin was killed during the attack on Pearl Harbor. Following his death, he was posthumously awarded the Purple Heart, and his family received a scroll signed by President Roosevelt honoring his memory. The scroll read:

> *In grateful memory of Laverne Alfred Austin who died in the service of his country at Pearl Harbor. T.H. attached U.S.S. Arizona, 7 December 1941. He stands in the unbroken line of patriots who have dared to die that freedom might live, and grow, and increase its blessings. Freedom lives, and through it, he lives—in a way that humbles the undertakings of most men.*

Robert Stratton

Birth: March 10, 1927, Smithfield, New York[611]
Death: February 21, 1945, Pacific Theater[612]
Burial: Remains Not Recovered; Memorialized, Courts of the Missing Honolulu Memorial, Hawaii

Robert Stratton grew up in Smithfield and Eaton and attended local schools. He entered the navy on his seventeenth birthday in March 1944. Upon completing his training at Great Lakes Training Station and Camp Shoemaker in California, he was assigned to the Pacific Theater. He was declared missing on February 21, 1945, when the ship he was on was attacked by suicide planes. Stratton was declared dead on June 16, 1945.

STOCKBRIDGE

Harry T. Cronin

Birth: July 16, 1923, New York[613]
Death: March 19, 1945, Germany[614]
Burial: St. Joseph Cemetery, Hamilton, New York

Harry Cronin attended Munnsville Schools and worked as a farmer and for Oneida Limited in the Knife Plant prior to enlisting in January 1943. He trained in the 294th Quartermaster Corps salvage repair company in North Carolina, Tennessee and New Jersey before being sent to the European Theater in September 1943.[615] He was killed in action in Germany; his remains were returned home in 1947.

Image taken from the Kenwood Chronicle. *Courtesy of the Oneida Community Mansion House.*

Lester W. Thurston

Birth: April 13, 1913, New York[616]
Death: November 17, 1944, France[617]
Burial: Stockbridge Cemetery, Stockbridge, New York

Lester Thurston grew up in Stockbridge and graduated from Stockbridge Valley Central School. Following graduation, he worked for the New York, Ontario and Western Railroad in Norwich. He joined the army in April 1942. He trained at Fort Bragg in North Carolina. He took part in campaigns in North Africa, Sicily, Italy and France. Thurston was killed in action in France. Thurston's remains were returned home in 1948.

SULLIVAN

James Lyndon Case

Birth: September 29, 1922, New York[618]
Death: March 1, 1945, Iwo Jima[619]
Burial: Oakwood Cemetery, Chittenango, New York

James Case grew up in Chittenango and graduated from Chittenango High School before enlisting in the Marine Corps in September 1942.[620] He was sent to Parris Island, South Carolina, for basic training and Camp Elliot in California, where he trained as a gunner for the Fleet Marine Force.[621] He was sent to New Zealand in February 1943 and then took part in the invasions of Bougainville, Guam and Iwo Jima.[622] He was promoted to corporal and received a Purple Heart after being injured on Guam. He was killed in action during the Battle of Iwo Jima. His remains were returned home in 1948.

Albert Desormeau

Birth: January 12, 1922, Canada[623]
Death: October 14, 1943, Italy
Burial: St. Agnes Cemetery, Chittenango, New York

Albert Desormeau's family moved around, but they were living in Chittenango in 1940. Desormeau joined the service shortly after the attacks on Pearl Harbor in December 1941. He trained at Fort Bragg, North Carolina, and was assigned to the Advance Chemical Warfare Unit.[624] He went overseas in the spring of 1943. He was killed in action during the invasion of Italy. His remains were returned home in November 1948.

Warren E. Hayward

Birth: February 11, 1922, Canastota, New York[625]
Death: July 11, 1944, off the coast of Italy[626]
Burial: Lost at Sea; Memorialized on the Tablet of the Missing, Sicily-Rome American Cemetery and Memorial Italy

Warren Hayward grew up in Lenox and Sullivan and enlisted in the navy in October 1940. Following his training, he earned the rank of coxswain and was assigned to the USS *Quincy*. Hayward was on the ship when it was sunk during the Battle of the Solomon Islands on August 9, 1942. He spent seven hours on a life raft with twenty-seven others waiting for rescue. Hayward lost everything except the clothes he was wearing. Eventually, they were rescued by a convoy and taken to the Solomon Islands. Following his rescue, he was furloughed for twenty days and returned home before returning to action and being assigned to the USS *Maddox*. He achieved the rank of torpedoman third class. In July 1944, Hayward was on the *Maddox* during the early morning hours when it was struck by several bombs from an enemy plane. He was originally reported missing in action, but by August, it was reported that he had died. A letter published in January 1944 sent by Lieutenant W.R. Laird Jr. to Warren's parents explained what happened:

> *I was the executive officer and senior surviving officer of the Maddox, and the Navy is permitting me to supply what little information is available.*
>
> *The Maddox was sunk fifteen miles off Sicily in the early morning of July 10. We were struck by several bombs from an enemy plane and severely damaged. The ship went down an hour before dawn.*
>
> *Your son was at his station on the depth charger when the bombs struck and although they hit in that part of the ship I could not find out if he was wounded by the bombs.*

After the ship went down all of us who are known to have survived were in the water about two hours before being rescued. As soon as we were picked up, the area was thoroughly searched but no additional survivors were found.

All hands had their life jackets on so it is believed that no one was lost who got in the water. I was sorry to have to report your son missing but I could find no trace of him when I mustered and questioned the survivors of the USS Maddox.[627]

JOHN H. KAY

Birth: December 5, 1916, Bergen, New York[628]
Death: October 25, 1945, Philippines
Burial: Crown Hill Memorial Park, Clinton, New York

John Kay's father was a Presbyterian minister who moved around a great deal. They settled in the Utica area, and Kay graduated from New Hartford High School in 1935. He then enrolled at Hamilton College in Clinton, New York, graduating in 1940. He enrolled at graduate school at Cornell University for two years before returning to Hamilton College to work as a lab assistant before taking a job as a chemist at the Holcomb Steel Plant in Syracuse. By this point in time, his family had moved to the town of Sullivan, and his father was the minister at churches in Wampsville and Chittenango. Kay entered the army in July 1942 and was sent overseas as part of the 886th Chemical Company in January 1943. He was attached to the 13th Air Force and was killed when the plane he was on crashed in the Island of Samar in the Philippines.[629] The plane was spraying trees with DDT. His remains were returned in 1948.

HARRY C. KINNETZ

Birth: March 18, 1908, Wampsville, New York[630]
Death: January 26, 1944, Italy[631]
Burial: Florence American Cemetery and Memorial, Lazio, Italy;
Memorial at Oakwood Cemetery, Chittenango, New York

Harry Kinnetz originally joined the army in 1926, serving three years in the Hawaiian Islands before returning to the Chittenango area in 1929. Following his return, he worked on power lines and as a farm laborer on his brother's farm. He reenlisted in the army in February 1942.[632] He worked as an instructor in the Mechanical Warfare Division at the Edgewood Arsenal in Maryland. He also served with a chemical battalion at Camp Gordon in Georgia. He obtained multiple promotions, earning the rank of staff sergeant at the time of his death. Kinnetz was listed as missing in action in Italy in March 1944.[633] A later notice said that he was killed in action.[634]

HAROLD E. SAGE

Birth: September 12, 1918, Buffalo, New York[635]
Death: July 26, 1943, Sicily[636]
Burial: Riverview Cemetery, Baldwinsville, New York

Harold Sage was working at Brown Lipe Chapin Company in Syracuse prior to the war. He married Fern Morse on December 12, 1941. The couple had one daughter, Harolin Elizabeth, who was born prematurely on August 31, 1943, and died one day later.[637] Their daughter is buried at Perryville Cemetery. Sage enlisted as a private in the army in February 1942. He trained at Camp Picket in Virginia and Pine Camp before going overseas and serving in North Africa and the invasion of Italy. He was killed in action. Sage was posthumously awarded the Purple Heart. His remains were returned home in 1949.[638]

PETER C. SLEIGHT

Birth: January 2, 1925, Rochester, New York[639]
Death: January 16, 1945, Belgium[640]
Burial: Newark Cemetery, New York

Peter Sleight graduated from Chittenango in 1943 and was already enrolled in the U.S. Army Air Corps. He initially trained as a meteorologist at Hamilton College before being transferred City College of New York. After spending a little over a month there, he was transferred to the infantry and trained at Camp Shelby in Mississippi. In December 1945, Sleight went overseas and was chosen as a replacement aide. He was reported missing in action in February 1945; in April of the same year, he was reported killed in action in Belgium. Sleight's remains were brought home in 1949.

Kenneth E. Winnie

Birth: January 5, 1923, Rochester, New York[641]
Death: May 24, 1945, Luzon
Burial: Oakwood Cemetery, Chittenango, New York

Kenneth Winnie graduated from Chittenango High School and enlisted in the army in March 1941.[642] He trained at Fort Slocum in New York and then was assigned to Hawaii. In a letter home from July 1941, he talked about the experience of the trip to Hawaii through the Panama Canal:

> *Had a grand trip down here. Went on board the SS Washington at Brooklyn Navy Yard. It took us six days to make Panama. Boy, are the docks something to see, especially the promenade deck of the Washington, the second largest ship in the United States!*
>
> *There are three sets of locks in the Panama Canal, Gatun, Peter Miguel and one other. After going through the canal about 40 miles and docked at Balboa; stayed there one night and entered the Pacific Ocean the next day. Four and a half days later we docked at San Francisco and were given shore leave. What a place! You need an overcoat at night and roast to death in the daytime.*
>
> *Then we were six days more reaching Pearl Harbor. There we went by train 27 miles up into the mountains to Schoffield Barracks where I am now. It costs $1 to go to Honolulu by taxi and 20 cents by bus.*
>
> *Have been to the Royal Hawaiian Hotel, Waikiki Beach and other famous resorts. Visited the volcano here. You can look straight down 200 feet and see the hot lava boiling. At another place, called the Paba, there is a cliff and when you get to the top you look down a sheer, solid rock wall for 700 feet. Several people have committed suicide by jumping off.*[643]

Winnie served in Pearl Harbor, New Guinea, Solomon Islands, Guadalcanal, Vella Avella and Luzon.[644] He was killed in action on Luzon. His remains were returned in August 1948.

Appendix

LISTED AS DECEASED BUT SURVIVED

GERALD "GILL" W. HOPKINS

Birth: July 14, 1890, Bouckville, New York[645]
Death: September 18, 1954, Syracuse, New York[646]
Burial: Unknown

Prior to the war, Gill Hopkins was working as a bottler at the Cider Mill in Bouckville[647] and later for Oneida Limited.[648] He was inducted as a private in the 153rd Depot Brigade on September 29, 1917.[649] He was transferred to the Second Company of the Ordnance Repair Shop in July 1918. In late August, he was sent overseas. Gill was listed as missing after the transport ship he was on (likely the USS *Mount Vernon*) was torpedoed in September 1918. He initially was listed as missing and was listed in a number of notices as "lost at sea." A second article informed his family that he arrived safely.[650] In 1919, he was included among the list of Madison County soldiers deceased. He was listed as being discharged on July 26, 1919.[651] Following the war, he returned to his job at Oneida Silversmiths as a cutting worker and machine operator.[652]

Robert Lasher

Birth: September 15, 1921, Chittenango, New York[653]
Death: May 3, 2018, Chittenango, New York[654]
Burial: Oakwood Cemetery, Chittenango, New York

Bob Lasher attended local schools and graduated from Chittenango High School in 1940.[655] He enlisted in the navy in July 1940 and, following training, was assigned to Pearl Harbor. He was on the USS *West Virginia* during the attack on December 7, 1941, and his family received notice that he was killed in action. Less than a week after receiving the first notice, a second was received that said the first was erroneous.[656] In the meantime, the family had prepared a memorial that became a thanksgiving for his being alive. Bob talked about his experiences during a recorded interview with the Madison County historian in 2013, including opening a letter in which his mother sent his obituary. This interview can be viewed at the Madison County website. When Bob returned home, he married Marian Miller in Chittenango on August 28, 1945. She passed away on October 14, 1999.

NOTES

Part I

1. "Draft Board Completes Work," *Madison County Times*, February 28, 1919, 2.
2. "The Local Board of Madison County," *Madison County's Welcome Home*, 1919, 77, via the *Oneida Dispatch Press*.
3. "The Food Administration," *Madison County's Welcome Home*, 1919, 83, via the *Oneida Dispatch Press*.
4. "Liberty Bonds and W.S.S.," *Madison County's Welcome Home*, 1919, 107, via the *Oneida Dispatch Press*.
5. "The Red Cross," *Madison County's Welcome Home*, 1919, 109, via the *Oneida Dispatch Press*.
6. "Colgate in the Great War," *Madison County's Welcome Home*, 1919, 85, via the *Oneida Dispatch Press*.
7. William M. Houghton, *History and Development, 1908–1968* (New York: State University of New York Agricultural and Technical College, 1968), 43–44. This self-published book is housed at the Madison County Historian's Office.
8. "Oneida Community, Ltd., What It Did in the War," *Madison County's Welcome Home*, 1919, 85, via the *Oneida Dispatch Press*.
9. "Jesse Lee Burdick," *Brookfield Courier*, October 26, 1921, 1.
10. New York Marriage Index, 1881–1967, "Jessie L. Burdick," http://www.ancestry.com.

11. New York, *Abstracts of World War I Military Service*, 1917–1919, "Curtis, Howard," http://www.ancestry.com.
12. "Buried with Military Honors; Private Howard Curtis, Who Was Killed in France, Buried at South Edmeston," *New Berlin Gazette*, July 23, 1921, 1.
13. Virginia, U.S., Death Records, 1912–2014, Meade Kenneth Palmer, http://www.ancestry.com.
14. "Meade Kenneth Palmer," *Brookfield Courier*, February 13, 1918, 1.
15. United States, World War I Draft Registration Cards, 1917–1918, "Carl Clarke Saunders," http://www.ancestry.com.
16. "Corporal Carl Saunders," *Brookfield Courier*, March 19, 1919, 2.
17. New York, *Abstracts of World War I Military Service*, 1917–1919, "Saunders, Carl C.," http://www.ancestry.com.
18. "Submarines Put Out of Business; Musician Carl Saunders Saw at Least Two Sent to Bottom," *Utica Herald Dispatch*, July 25, 1918, 10.
19. "Letter from Carl Saunders," *Brookfield Courier*, March 19, 1919, 1.
20. "Charles Bevines Vunk," *Brookfield Courier*, March 5, 1919, 1.
21. "Hubert William Butts," *Cazenovia Republican*, October 31, 1918, New Woodstock Section, 1.
22. United States, World War I Draft Registration Cards, 1917–1918, "Arthur Herbert Reeves," http://www.ancestry.com.
23. "Arthur H Reeves Dies in Camp," *Cazenovia Republican*, October 24, 1918, 1.
24. New York Marriage Index, 1881–1967, "Arthur H. Reeves," http://www.ancestry.com.
25. Virginia, Death Records, 1912–2014, "Arthur H Reeve," http://www.ancestry.com.
26. New York, *Abstracts of World War I Military Service*, 1917–1919, "Branagan, Andrew," http://www.ancestry.com.
27. New York, State Census, "Enumeration of the Inhabitants of West Eaton, Madison County," 8, 1915, http://www.ancestry.com.
28. "Leland Mead Dies at Front; Succumbed on October 4th to Wounds Received in Battle," *Madison County Leader and Observer*, November 14, 1918, 1.
29. "Death of the Mead Brothers; First Details Regarding Their Killing," *Madison County Leader and Observer*, April 10, 1919, 1.
30. New York, *Abstracts of World War I Military Service*, 1917–1919, "Mead, Theodore Fletcher," http://www.ancestry.com.
31. "Dr. Mead Dead in France; Killed Oct. 30th While Giving Aid to Wounded," *Madison County Leader and Observer*, November 28, 1918, 1.

32. "Had His Share of 'Thrills': Dr. (now Captain) Theodore F. Mead Writes Interestingly of His Experiences at the Front," *Madison County Leader and Observer*, November 21, 1918, 1.
33. "Death of the Mead Brothers," 1.
34. United States, World War I Draft Registration Cards, 1917–1918, "Jasper Smith," http://www.ancestry.com.
35. "Private Jasper Smith Dead in France, Wounded by Shrapnel-Died of Pneumonia," *Madison County Leader and Observer*, November 21, 1918, 8.
36. New York, State Census, "Enumeration of the Inhabitants of Eaton, Madison County," 7, 1915, http://www.ancestry.com.
37. New York, *Abstracts of World War I Military Service*, 1917–1919, "Smith, Jasper," http://www.ancestry.com.
38. "Private Jasper Smith," 8.
39. New York, *Abstracts of World War I Military Service*, 1917–1919, "Westcott, Percy Douane," http://www.ancestry.com.
40. "Experiences as a TAR; Attack of Measles and Then Mumps, Introduction to US Marine Service in France," *Madison County Leader and Observer*, October 18, 1917, 1.
41. "Letter from Percy Westcott; Young Soldier Writes that January Weather in France Is Like Our April," *Madison County Leader and Observer*, March 21, 1918, 5.
42. "Letter from France; Percy D. Westcott of Eaton Writes to Friend in Hamilton," *Madison County Leader and Observer*, September 26, 1918, 3.
43. United States, World War I Draft Registration Cards, 1917–1918, "Lloyd Henry Stoker," http://www.ancestry.com.
44. *Akron City Directory*, 1917, 1,720; 1918, 1,348.
45. Ohio Soldiers in World War I, 1917–1918, "Lloyd H. Stoker," http://www.ancestry.com.
46. *Colgate University General Catalogue Number*, vol. 2, ed. Elmer William Smith, 1916.
47. "Local Items About Our Own People," *Hamilton Republican*, March 14, 1918, 5.
48. "Lieut. Anderson Missing in Action; Fails to Return from Flight Over German Lines," *Hamilton Republican*, August 22, 1918, 1.
49. New York, *Abstracts of World War I Military Service*, 1917–1919, "Baker, Robert Blaine," http://www.ancestry.com.
50. "Robert Blaine Baker Dies in the Service; Former Colgate and Earlville Resident Victim of Pneumonia," *Hamilton Republican*, October 17, 1918, 1.

51. "Robert Blaine Baker; Final Tribute to the Memory of a True Soldier and Friend," *Earlville Standard*, October 17, 1918, 1.
52. United States, World War I Draft Registration Cards, 1917–1918, "Brown, William," http://www.ancestry.com.
53. "William Brown Died in France; News Recently Received, Details the Manner of His Death," *Hamilton Republican*, May 29, 1919, 1.
54. U.S. Census Bureau, 1900, *Twelfth Census of the United States: 1900—Population*, "District 12-3, Brookfield, Madison County, New York," Sheet 3, http://www.ancestry.com.
55. "Poolville," *Earlville Standard*, April 25, 1918, 8.
56. "Local Matters," *Brookfield Courier*, August 26, 1914, 3.
57. New York, *Abstracts of World War I Military Service*, 1917–1919, "Cockett, Ray Ducher," http://www.ancestry.com.
58. "Raymond Cockett Buried with Military Honors," *Earlville Standard*, May 2, 1918, 1.
59. United States, World War I Draft Registration Cards, 1917–1918, "Vinton A Dearning," http://www.ancestry.com.
60. "Lieut. Vinton Dearing Killed; Falls While Fighting on Western Front," *Hamilton Republican*, August 22, 1918, 1.
61. "Late Lieutenant Dearing; Honored by General Pershing," *Hamilton Republican*, September 12 1918, 1.
62. "Lieutenant Dearing Killed; Massachusetts Man, Graduate of Colgate, Sent Message to Mother," *Utica Herald Dispatch*, September 12, 1918, 5.
63. "Lloyd V. Evans of the US Marines Killed in France," *Madison County Leader and Observer*, July 4, 1918, 3.
64. "News from the Trenches," *Hamilton Republican*, May 16, 1918, 1.
65. "Lloyd Evans Sends Word from France," *Hamilton Republican*, June 13, 1918, 1.
66. New York, *Abstracts of World War I Military Service*, 1917–1919, "Hawkinson, Howard Edwards," http://www.ancestry.com.
67. "Captain Howard E Hawkinson, One of the First Syracusans to Enter the…Died a Hero One Month Before the Armistice; Was in Bloodiest Fights," *Syracuse Herald*, June 1, 1919, 8.
68. Ohio Soldiers in World War I, 1917–1918, "Michael J. Hays," http://www.ancestry.com.
69. "Five Colgate Men Killed in Action; Give Their Lives During Final Month of Fighting," *Hamilton Republican*, November 28, 1918, 4.
70. "MICHAEL J HAYES," Part 2, *New York Herald*, February 14, 1919, 5.

71. "First Camden Boy to Fall on Battlefield; Sergt. Arthur S. Moran Makes Supreme Sacrifice," *Camden Advance Journal*, November 21, 1918, 1.
72. "Five Colgate Men Killed in Action Give Their Lives During Final Month of Fighting," *Hamilton Republican*, November 28, 1918, 4.
73. New York, *Abstracts of World War I Military Service*, 1917–1919, "Moran, Arthur Seward," http://www.ancestry.com.
74. "First Camden Boy to Fall on Battlefield."
75. "Community Meets in Memory of Sergeant S. Moran," *Camden Advance-Journal*, January 9, 1919, 1.
76. New York, *Abstracts of World War I Military Service*, 1917–1919, "Naughton, Harold LeRoy," http://www.ancestry.com.
77. "Capt. Harold L. Naughton Killed; His Widow Receives Official Word from the War Department," *Watertown Times*, November 13, 1918, 12.
78. "Capt. Naughton Shot in Shoulder; Wound Was Not Believed to Be Serious; Story of Battle Told," *Watertown Daily Times*, February 8, 1919, 5.
79. "Glenn Newland Satterlee; Second Hamilton Boy to Make the Supreme Sacrifice," *Hamilton Republican*, October 10, 1918, 1.
80. "Hamilton Boys in Service; Two Sons of Mr. and Mrs. C.E. Satterlee on the Other Side," *Hamilton Republican*, May 30, 1918, 1.
81. New York, *Abstracts of World War I Military Service*, 1917–1919, "Connell, Luther C.," http://www.ancestry.com.
82. "Over Top Three Times; Not Hurt," *Syracuse Herald*, September 12, 1918, 16.
83. U.S. Veterans Administration Master Index, 1917–1940, "Carl Louis Lynder Foote," http://www.ancestry.com.
84. New York, *Abstracts of World War I Military Service*, 1917–1919, "Foote, Carl L.," http://www.ancestry.com.
85. New York, State Census, "Enumeration of the Inhabitants of Canastota, Madison County," 4, 1915, http://www.ancestry.com.
86. "Killed at Chauteau Thierry," *Oneida Democratic Union*, November 28, 1918, 1.
87. "How Carl Foote Died," *Canastota Courant*, November 29, 1918, 1.
88. New York, *World War I Veterans' Service Data*, 1913–1919, "Eliphalet S. Houghton," http://www.ancestry.com.
89. Michigan, Death Records, 1867–1952, "Letha E Haighton," http://www.ancestry.com.
90. "Canastota Man Dead in France," *Canastota Bee Journal*, October 11, 1919, 1.

91. "Carlton Lower Killed in Action; Sad News Reaches Canastota Relatives Wednesday," *Canastota Bee Journal*, December 14, 1918, 1.
92. New York, *Abstracts of World War I Military Service*, 1917–1919, "Lower, Carlton A.," http://www.ancestry.com.
93. New York, *World War I Veterans' Service Data*, 1913–1919, "Carlton A. Lower," http://www.ancestry.com.
94 "Charles Miller Killed in Action; Telegram Received by Grandfather Thursday," *Canastota Bee*, August 10, 1918, 1.
95. "Made Supreme Sacrifice," *Madison County Times*, August 16, 1918, 3.
96. United States, World War I Draft Registration Cards, 1917–1918, "Joel Northrup Waterbury," http://www.ancestry.com.
97. New York, *Abstracts of World War I Military Service*, 1917–1919, "Waterbury, Joel N.," http://www.ancestry.com.
98. New York, *Abstracts of World War I Military Service*, 1917–1919, "Wilson, George H.," http://www.ancestry.com.
99. New York, *World War I Veterans' Service Data*, 1913–1919, "George H. Wilson," http://www.ancestry.com.
100. United States, World War I Draft Registration Cards, 1917–1918, "Nicholas A Gregg," http://www.ancestry.com.
101. New York, *Abstracts of World War I Military Service*, 1917–1919, "Gregg, Nicholas A.," http://www.ancestry.com.
102. New York, State Census, "Enumeration of the Inhabitants of Fenner, Madison County," 4, 1915, http://www.ancestry.com.
103. "Hero's Body Laid at Rest," *Madison County Times*, September 30, 1921, 3.
104. "County and Neighboring; Items Concerning This Vicinity and Elsewhere," *Hamilton Republican*, February 14, 1918, 8.
105. *Madison County Leader and Observer*, October 12, 1916, 8.
106. New York, *Abstracts of World War I Military Service*, 1917–1919, "Downey, Stephen John," http://www.ancestry.com.
107. "Schenectadian Is Killed When Ship Is Sunk by Sub; Stephen J. Downey, Who Enlisted in Navy Last Winter, Teuton Victim," *Schenectady Gazette*, January 30, 1918, 4.
108. "Belated Announcement of the Death of Stephen Downey," *Waterville Times*, November 16, 1917, 1.
109. "Schenectadian Is Killed When Ship Is Sunk by Sub."
110. United States, World War I Draft Registration Cards, 1917–1918, "Lynn E Kelly," http://www.ancestry.com.

111. "Bouckville," *Madison County Leader and Observer*, May 29, 1919, 8.
112. New York, *Abstracts of World War I Military Service*, 1917–1919, "Kelly, Lynn E.," http://www.ancestry.com.
113. New York, *Abstracts of World War I Military Service*, 1917–1919, "Kelsey, Louis Francis," http://www.ancestry.com.
114. "Death of Rev. Louis F. Kelsey—The New Grange Officers," *Madison County Leader and Observer*, January 23, 1919, 8.
115. New York Marriage Index, 1881–1967, "Louis F Kelsey," http://www.ancestry.com.
116. "Rev. L.F. Kelsey Is Hurt Serving on Battle Line; Former Cicero Pastor Now Recovering in French Hospital," *Post-Standard*, September 19, 1918, 7.
117. "Erieville," *DeRuyter Gleaner*, August 7, 1919, 1.
118. New York, *Abstracts of World War I Military Service*, 1917–1919, "Alger, Earl R.," http://www.ancestry.com.
119. New York, State Census, "Enumeration of the Inhabitants of Lowville, Lewis County," 16, 1915, http://www.ancestry.com.
120. "The Late H.L. Armstrong; Details Regarding His Army Career and Duties in France," *Rome Daily Sentinel*, December 11, 1918, 6.
121. "Herbert L. Armstrong," *Oneida Democratic Union*, December 19, 1918, 1.
122. New York, *Abstracts of World War I Military Service*, 1917–1919, "Armstrong, Herbert L.," http://www.ancestry.com.
123. United States, World War I Draft Registration Cards, 1917–1918, "Wells C Cochran," http://www.ancestry.com.
124. "Wells Cochran," *Oneida Democratic Union*, October 3, 1918, 1.
125. New York, *Abstracts of World War I Military Service*, 1917–1919, "Cochran, Wells C.," http://www.ancestry.com.
126. New York Birth Index, 1881–1942, "Percy A. Dean," http://www.ancestry.com.
127. New York, *Abstracts of World War I Military Service*, 1917–1919, "Dean, Percy A.," http://www.ancestry.com.
128. New York, State Census, "Enumeration of the Inhabitants of Ward 3 of Oneida, Madison County," 12, 1915, http://www.ancestry.com.
129. "Will Have Military Honors," *Utica Herald-Dispatch*, October 21, 1921, 26.
130. United States, World War I Draft Registration Cards, 1917–1918, "James Bernard Dunn," http://www.ancestry.com.
131. U.S. Census Bureau, 1910, *Thirteenth Census of the United States: 1910—Population*, "District 29, Oneida Ward 4, Madison County, New York," Sheet 13A, http://www.ancestry.com.

132. New York, State Census, "Enumeration of the Inhabitants of Ward 4 of Oneida, Madison County," 13, 1915, http://www.ancestry.com.
133. "Fiancé Falls, Hun Victim," *Syracuse Journal*, October 12, 1918, 6.
134. "Bernie Dunn," *Oneida Democratic Union*, October 10, 1918, 1.
135. United States, World War I Draft Registration Cards, 1917–1918, "Cecil Thurston Ernenwein," http://www.ancestry.com.
136. "Soldier Dies of Diphtheria," *Oneida Democratic Union*, January 17, 1918, 5.
137. New York, *Abstracts of World War I Military Service*, 1917–1919, "Ernenwein, Cecil T.," http://www.ancestry.com.
138. United States, World War I Draft Registration Cards, 1917–1918, "Martin Girolamo," http://www.ancestry.com.
139. "Martino Geralamo, First Soldier from Oneida to Be Killed in World War," *Oneida Democratic Union*, May 23, 1918, 1.
140. New York Marriage Index, 1881–1967, "Martino Girolamo," http://www.ancestry.com.
141. New York, Death Index, 1852–1956, "Catharine Giorlamo," http://www.ancestry.com.
142. United States, World War I Draft Registration Cards, 1917–1918, "Elon Eugene Hill," http://www.ancestry.com.
143. U.S. Census Bureau, 1910, *Thirteenth Census of the United States: 1910—Population*, "District 31, Oneida, Madison County, New York," Sheet 1A, http://www.ancestry.com.
144. New York, State Census, "Enumeration of the Inhabitants of Verona, Oneida County," 3, 1915, http://www.ancestry.com.
145. United States, World War I Draft Registration Cards, 1917–1918, "Elon Eugene Hill," http://www.ancestry.com.
146. "For Their Country's Sake; Six Madison Co. Boys Answer Last Roll Call," *Madison County Times*, October 18, 1918, 2.
147. "Killed at St. Mihiel; Elon Hill's Death Confirmed by His Captain—Died Bravely," *Oneida Democratic Union*, January September 1919, 1.
148. New York, *Abstracts of World War I Military Service*, 1917–1919, "Hinds, Elliot P.," http://www.ancestry.com.
149. U.S. Census Bureau, 1910, *Thirteenth Census of the United States: 1910—Population*, "District 105, Niagara Falls Ward 3, Niagara County, New York," Sheet 17A, http://www.ancestry.com.
150. "Elliot P. Hinds Killed," *Oneida Dispatch*, July 12, 1918, 5.
151. Massachusetts, Birth Record, 1840–1915, "Sheldon C Houston," http://www.ancestry.com.

152. "Killed in France; Sheldon Houston of Oneida Castle Killed Nov. 3—News Just Received Here," *Oneida Democratic Union*, March 27, 1919, 4.
153. U.S. Census Bureau, 1910, *Thirteenth Census of the United States: 1910—Population*, "District 22, Haworth, Bergen County, New Jersey," Sheet 6A, http://www.ancestry.com.
154. New York, *Abstracts of World War I Military Service*, 1917–1919, "Johnston, Claude Raymond," http://www.ancestry.com.
155. "Claude Johnston," *Oneida Democratic Union*, October 31, 1918, 1.
156. "Body Arrives Home; Claude Johnston Died in England, Funeral Saturday," *Oneida Democratic Union*, December 12, 1918, 1.
157. Ibid.
158. United States, World War I Draft Registration Cards, 1917–1918, "Daniel H. Kinney," http://www.ancestry.com.
159. New York, *Abstracts of World War I Military Service*, 1917–1919, "Kinney, Daniel H.," http://www.ancestry.com.
160. "Died in France; Daniel Kinney of Oneida Died February 12th from Flu, at Semur," *Oneida Democratic Union*, March 27, 1919, 4.
161. New York, *Abstracts of World War I Military Service*, 1917–1919. "Koch, Ernest G," http://www.ancestry.com.
162. "For Their County's Sake; Ernest Koch of Oneida Dies in France," *Madison County Times*, October 25, 1918, 3.
163. New York, *Abstracts of World War I Military Service*, 1917–1919, "Uebelacker, Lawrence," http://www.ancestry.com.
164. United States, World War I Draft Registration Cards, 1917–1918, "Asa Cranston Vedder," http://www.ancestry.com.
165. U.S. Census Bureau, 1910, *Thirteenth Census of the United States: 1910—Population*, "District 32, Smithfield, Madison County, New York," Sheet 7A, http://www.ancestry.com.
166. New York, *Abstracts of World War I Military Service*, 1917–1919, "Vedder, Asa C.," http://www.ancestry.com.
167. "Asa Vedder of Fenner Gased and Dies in Hospital," *Cazenovia Republican*, October 17, 1918.
168. "The Body of Corp. Samuel Bovee, Who Gave His Life for Freedom, Rests in a French Cemetery," *Madison County Leader and Observer*, November 28, 1918, 8.
169. New York, *Abstracts of World War I Military Service*, 1917–1919, "Bovee, Samuel Arthur," http://www.ancestry.com.
170. "Stockbridge Boy Killed in France," *Oneida Dispatch*, July 12, 1918, 1.

171. United States, World War I Draft Registration Cards, 1917–1918, "Horace Elmer Davenport," http://www.ancestry.com.
172. U.S. Census Bureau, *Thirteenth Census of the United States: 1910—Population*, "Stockbridge Town," April 18, 1910, Sheet No. 1B, www.ancestry.com.
173. "Horace E Davenport," *Oneida Democratic Union*, July 11, 1918, 1.
174. New York, *Abstracts of World War I Military Service*, 1917–1919, "Davenport, Horace Elmer," http://www.ancestry.com.
175. United States, World War I Draft Registration Cards, 1917–1918, "George Harrison Northing," http://www.ancestry.com.
176. New York, *Abstracts of World War I Military Service*, 1917–1919, "Northing, George H.," http://www.ancestry.com.
177. "George H. Northing Killed in Action," *Madison County Times*, March July 1919, 2.
178. New York, *Abstracts of World War I Military Service*, 1917–1919, "Sayles, Claude Elmer," http://www.ancestry.com.
179. U.S. Census Bureau, 1900, *Twelfth Census of the United States: 1900—Population*, "District 67, Warren, Herkimer County, New York," Sheet 1A, http://www.ancestry.com.
180. U.S. Census Bureau, 1910, *Thirteenth Census of the United States: 1910—Population*, "District 83, Fort Plain, Montgomery County, New York," Sheet 2, http://www.ancestry.com.
181. "Claude E. Sayles; Syracuse Boy, a Marine, Who Was Killed in Action June 6th," *Syracuse Herald*, July 23, 1918, 14.
182. Ibid.
183. New York, *Abstracts of World War I Military Service*, 1917–1919, "Wheeler, John E.," http://www.ancestry.com.
184. "John E. Wheeler," *Madison County Times*, March 29, 1918, 2.

Part II

185. "2 Cazenovians on County Draft Boards," *Cazenovia Republican*, September 26, 1940, 1.
186. "Campbell Names Area Draft Board," *Rome Daily Sentinel*, September 24, 1940, 6.
187. "News Notes," *Rome Sentinel*, September 13, 1945, 6.
188. "'E' Award Given to Laboratories," *Rome Sentinel*, May 19, 1945, 6.
189. United States, World War II Draft Cards, 1940–1947, "Norman Wesley Ballard," http://www.ancestry.com.

190. "Sgt. N.W. Ballard Reported Killed; Former Resident Lost in France; Worked in Rome for Revere," *Rome Daily Sentinel*, September 28, 1944, 17.
191. "Leonardsville Department," *Brookfield Courier*, November 16, 1944, 8.
192. "Leonardsville," *A Book of Remembrance*, from the Wives and Mothers Club, 84.
193. "North Brookfield," *A Book of Remembrance*, from the Wives and Mothers Club, 20.
194. U.S. Census Bureau, 1940, *Sixteenth Census of the United States: 1940—Population*, "District 41-724, New York, Queens County, New York," Sheet 1A, http://www.ancestry.com.
195. "Erford Johnson Dies Prisoner of War in Philippine Islands," *DeRuyter Gleaner*, August 2, 1945, 5.
196. "Legion Post Will Bear Name of Johnson-Rogers," *Brookfield Courier*, July 18, 1946, 1.
197. United States, World War II Draft Cards, 1940–1947, "Harold Edwin Loomis," http://www.ancestry.com.
198. "Memorial Service for SGT. Harold Loomis," *Brookfield Courier*, August 31, 1944, 5.
199. U.S. Census Bureau, 1940, *Sixteenth Census of the United States: 1940—Population*, "District 27-34, Madison, Madison County, New York," Sheet 5A, http://www.ancestry.com.
200. "Lieut. Dighton Polan Killed in Action; First Casualty in New Berlin's List of Service Men," *New Berlin Gazette*, November 26, 1942, 1.
201. United States, World War II Draft Cards, 1940–1947, "Douglass Irving Rice," http://www.ancestry.com.
202. "Post Rites for Douglas Irving Rice," *Brookfield Courier*, February 3, 1949, 1.
203. "Douglas Rice Dies in Service," *Brookfield Courier*, August 9, 1945, 1.
204. "Post Rites for Douglass Irving Rice," 1.
205. "Death at a Hero's Station; Ilion Machinist Caught in Torpedo Explosion," *Utica Observer Dispatch*, July 27, 1943, 4A.
206. "Brookfield," *A Book of Remembrance*, from the Wives and Mothers Club, 13.
207. "Memorial Service for Royce Rogers," *Brookfield Courier*, April 5, 1945, 1.
208. "Body of Pfc. Stone Arrives Tuesday; Services Wednesday," *Chenango Union* (Norwich, NY), January 6, 1949, 1.
209. "PFC. Hugh Stone Jr. Dead in England," *Brookfield Courier*, November 3, 1943, 5.

210. "Brookfield," *Book of Remembrance*, 12.
211. "PFC. Elmer Wheeler Dies in France," *Brookfield Courier*, August 3, 1944, 1.
212. "West Eaton," *A Book of Remembrance*, from the Wives and Mothers Club, 47.
213. "Private Wheeler Buried in Clinton," *Utica Daily Press*, May 31, 1948, 9.
214. "Unadilla Forks Soldier Killed in Luxembourg," *Otsego Farmer*, March 2, 1945, 3.
215. "Leonardsville," *Book of Remembrance*, 85.
216. New York Birth Index, 1881–1942, "Donald W. Aldrich," http://www.ancestry.com.
217. "Additions to Cayuga County Casualty List; Young Marine Falls on Iwo," *Citizen Advertiser*, April 14, 1945, 5.
218. "New Woodstock Army Flier Is Killed in Action," *Canastota Bee-Journal*, July 14, 1944, 1.
219. United States, World War II Draft Cards, 1940–1947. "Louis Wilson Buckingham," http://www.ancestry.com.
220. "Cpl. Louis Buckingham of New Woodstock Killed in Action," *Cazenovia Republican*, December 21, 1944, 1.
221. "Funeral Services for Cpl. Buckingham Will Be Held," *DeRuyter Gleaner*, June 9, 1949, 1.
222. "Pvt. Arthur Lewis Bush of Sheds Killed in Action January 18, While Serving with 1st Army in Belgium," *DeRuyter Gleaner*, March 15, 1945, 1.
223. United States, World War II Draft Cards, 1940–1947, "Eugene Kenneth Cook," http://www.ancestry.com.
224. "Pvt. Eugene Cook Dies from Wounds Received in France," *Cazenovia Republican*, November 9, 1944, 4.
225. United States, World War II Draft Cards, 1940–1947, "Donald Maise Davis," http://www.ancestry.com.
226. "Lt. Donald M. Davis Dies in Florida," *Cazenovia Republican*, July 8, 1943, 4.
227. "Rites Held at Cazenovia for Lt. Donald M. Davis," *Syracuse Herald-Journal*, July 15, 1943, 16.
228. "Lt. Wm. Haines Dies Fighting in France," *Cazenovia Republican*, August 31, 1944, 1.
229. "Lt. William G. Haines, Jr. Killed in France Aug. 13," *Syracuse Herald Journal*, August 31, 1944, 13.
230. "Lt. William G. Haines Jr., USA," *Cazenovia Republican*, June 8, 1944, 4.

231. Ibid., 13.
232. "Sgt. Bruce Jenkins Killed in Action in Battle of Luzon," *DeRuyter Gleaner*, February 22, 1945, 6.
233. "Memorial Services for S/Sgt. Bruce Jenkins," *Cazenovia Republican*, May 17, 1945, 4.
234. "PFC Bruce E. Jenkins," *Cazenovia Republican*, November 11, 1943, 4.
235. United States, World War II Draft Cards, 1940–1947, "Howard Ray Lieurance," http://www.ancestry.com.
236. *Cazenovia Republican*, November 18, 1943.
237. "Lieurance-Berrena," *Cazenovia Republican*, January 7, 1943, 4.
238. "Service Cross Is Awarded to Lt. Lieurance Posthumously," *Cazenovia Republican*, May 11, 1944, 1.
239. Ibid.
240. United States, World War II Draft Cards, 1940–1947, "Thomas McNulty," http://www.ancestry.com.
241. "Services Conducted for T/Sgt. McNulty," *Cazenovia Republican*, May 4, 1950, 6.
242. U.S. Census Bureau, 1940, *Sixteenth Census of the United States: 1940—Population*, "District 89-151, Minneapolis, Hennepin County, New York," Sheet 96B, http://www.ancestry.com.
243. "Services Conducted."
244. United States, World War II Draft Cards, 1940–1947, "Edward Olcott Miller," http://www.ancestry.com.
245. "T-5 Edward Miller Who Died Overseas Funeral Sunday," *Cazenovia Republican*, November 25, 1948, 6.
246. "News from Our Boys," *Cazenovia Republican*, February 24, 1944, 4.
247. "T-5 Edward Miller."
248. "New Woodstock News Department," *DeRuyter Gleaner*, December 21, 1944, 6.
249. United States, World War II Draft Cards, 1940–1947, "Albert John Potter," http://www.ancestry.com.
250. "News from Our Boys," *Cazenovia Republican*, September 28, 1944, 8.
251. "Potter-Morgan," *Cazenovia Republican*, August 12, 1943, 4.
252. "Memorial Services for Lt. Potter," *Cazenovia Republican*, March 15, 1945, 4.
253. "Malcolm S Taylor," *Cazenovia Republican*, May 20, 1943, 3.
254. U.S. Census Bureau, 1940, *Sixteenth Census of the United States: 1940—Population*, "District 27-7, Cazenovia, Madison County, New York," Sheet 3B, http://www.ancestry.com.

255. "Prt. Eric Trammell Dies After Wounds Received in France," *Cazenovia Republican*, January 18, 1945, 1.
256. "Funeral Services for Pvt. Fred L. Waffner," *Tully Times*, June 24, 1948, 1.
257. New York Birth Index, 1881–1942, "Frederick L. Waffner," http://www.ancestry.com.
258. "Last Rites for Pvt. F.L. Waffner," *DeRuyter Gleaner*, July 1, 1948, 1.
259. United States, World War II Draft Cards, 1940–1947, "Bernard Joseph Works," http://www.ancestry.com.
260. "Pvt. Bernard J. Works Killed in Action July 10 in France," *Cazenovia Republican*, August 3, 1944, 1.
261. "Born to Mrs. Bernard J. Works," *Cazenovia Republican*, December 14, 1944, 5.
262. "Pvt. James H. Hinds of DeRuyter Makes Supreme Sacrifice for His Country, Somewhere in Germany," *DeRuyter Gleaner*, April 12, 1945, 1.
263. "Letter of Condolence," *DeRuyter Gleaner*, May 10, 1945, 5.
264. "Last Rites for DeRuyter's First World War II, Dead," *DeRuyter Gleaner*, June 10, 1948, 1.
265. "Memorial Service for Lt. Harlow M. Truman," *Brookfield Courier*, May 17, 1945, 1.
266. "Memorial Service for Lt. Harlow M. Truman to Be Held Here Sunday," *DeRuyter Gleaner*, May 17, 1945, 1.
267. New York Birth Index, 1881–1942, "Charles W. Clark," http://www.ancestry.com.
268. "Lieutenant Clark Killed in Action by Enemy Plane," *Madison County Leader and Observer*, October 12, 1944, 1.
269. "Two Madison Co. Fliers Reported Missing in Flights Over Europe," *Madison County Times*, April 14, 1944, 4.
270. "Killed on Mission –Over Germany," *Madison County Times*, October 12, 1944, 5.
271. United States, World War II Draft Cards, 1940–1947, "Michael Denega," http://www.ancestry.com.
272. "T/5 M. Denega Killed Jan. 12," *Rome Daily Sentinel*, February 21, 1945, 6.
273. World War II Draft Cards, "Michael Denega."
274. New York Marriage Index, 1881–1967, "Shirley Church," http://www.ancestry.com.
275. "Eaton," *A Book of Remembrance*, from the Wives and Mothers Club, 41.

276. "Pvt. Alan Mosher Former Resident Killed in France," *DeRuyter Gleaner*, January 25, 1945, 5.
277. United States, World War II Army Enlistment Records, 1938–1946, "Alan H. Mosher," http://www.ancestry.com.
278. New York Birth Index, 1881–1942, "Francis H. Sisbower," http://www.ancestry.com.
279. "West Eaton," *Book of Remembrance*, 47.
280. Florida State Census, 1867–1945 (1935), "Francis H. Sisbower," http://www.ancestry.com.
281. North Carolina Birth Indexes, 1800–2000, "Joyce Dean Sisbower," http://www.ancestry.com.
282. Ibid.
283. "West Eaton," *Book of Remembrance*, 47.
284. United States, World War II Draft Cards, 1940–1947, "Edward Richard Smith," http://www.ancestry.com.
285. "Seaman Smith Killed in Action; Mother Learns Death Resulted from Accidental Explosion in Pacific Area," *Rome Daily Sentinel*, June 8, 1944, 7.
286. "Morrisville," *A Book of Remembrance*, from the Wives and Mothers Club, 107.
287. "Died from Fever in Leyte Hospital," *Madison County Times*, February 23, 1945, 5.
288. "S/Sgt. Howard Smith," *Brookfield Courier*, February 15, 1945, 6.
289. "West Eaton," *Book of Remembrance*, 47.
290. "Rites Slated for Sgt. Smith," *Utica Daily Press*, August 18, 1948, 16.
291. "Funeral Services for Ralph A. Snyder Held at Newark Valley Home," Madison County Leader, February 15, 1945, 1.
292. Pennsylvania Marriages, 1852–1968, "Ralph A Snyder," http://www.ancestry.com.
293. "Memorial Services Held for Corp Westcott," *Brookfield Courier*, June 28, 1945, 6.
294. "West Eaton," *Book of Remembrance*, 47.
295. United States, World War II Draft Cards, 1940–1947, "Albert Richard Wilt," http://www.ancestry.com.
296. "Lt. Albert Wilt Officially Listed Dead," *Madison County Leader and Observer*, December 7, 1944, 1.
297. "Hope Express that Lt. A.R. Wilt May Still Be Alive," *Madison County Leader and Observer*, June 15, 1944, 1.
298. "Lt. Albert Wilt," 1.

299. United States, World War II Draft Cards, 1940–1947, "Edmund Joseph Burke," http://www.ancestry.com.
300. "Former Utican Now Presumed Dead, 5 Area Soldiers Wounded in Action," *Utica Daily Press*, November 19, 1944, 6-A.
301. "Another Perryville Boy Reported Missing in Action," *Cazenovia Republican*, October 14, 1943, 4.
302. "Former Utican," 6-A.
303. United States, World War II Draft Cards, 1940–1947, "Grant Clifton Schaff," http://www.ancestry.com.
304. "S/Sgt. Grant Schaff Missing Over Year, Declared Dead," *Cazenovia Republican*, August 31, 1944, 8.
305. "S/Sgt. Grant Schaff, Cazenovia Graduate, Missing in Action," *Cazenovia Republican*, August 12, 1943, 4.
306. "S/Sgt. Grant Schaff Missing Over Year," 8.
307. United States, World War II Draft Cards, 1940–1947, "Bernard Charles Seitz," http://www.ancestry.com.
308. "Service Cross Citation Reach G. Seitz Family; Corporal Bernard C. Seitz, Oneida, Posthumously Honored by War Department," *Oneida Daily Dispatch*, November 2, 1942, 3.
309. "Corp. Bernard C. Seitz, Oneida, Reported Missing," *Oneida Daily Dispatch*, June 22, 1942, 1.
310. "Service Cross Citation," 3.
311. United States, World War II Draft Cards, 1940–1947, "Henry William Seitz, Jr.," http://www.ancestry.com.
312. "Canastotan Is Killed in Plane Crash; Lt. Henry W. Seitz, Jr., Loses Life in Accident in California," *Syracuse Herald-Journal*, August 8, 1944, 6.
313. United States, Headstone Application for Military Veterans, 1925–1963, "Henry W. Seitz, Jr.," http://www.ancestry.com.
314. United States, World War II Draft Cards, 1940–1947, "Frederick Jerome Sherman," http://www.ancestry.com.
315. "Killed in France," *DeRuyter Gleaner*, November 2, 1944, 7.
316. New York Birth Index, 1881–1942, "Wilfred S. Trass," http://www.ancestry.com.
317. "Memorial Services at School," *DeRuyter Gleaner*, May 24, 1945, 2.
318. "Tommy Bates, Grandson of Late Mayor, Dies in Action; Only Son of Mr. and Mrs. Stanley Bates Was Member of Rangers after Transfer from Assignment with Ski Troops," *Quincy Patriot Ledger*, February 14, 1944, 1.
319. "Lt. Bates Met Death Just Before His 23rd Birthday," *Quincy Patriot Ledger*, April 21, 1944, 7.

320. United States, World War II Draft Cards, 1940–1947, "Barclay Boyd Beeby," http://www.ancestry.com.
321. "Lt. Boyd Beeby Killed in Crash in Puerto Rico; Flying Hero Dies in Forced Landing of Superfortress," *Alton Evening Telegraph*, January 2, 1945, 1.
322. Missouri, Marriage Records, 1805–2002, "Boyd Beeby," http://www.ancestry.com.
323. "Lt. Boyd Beeby Killed in Crash in Puerto Rico," 1.
324. "Barclay B. Beeby, Silver Star," Military Times, https://valor.militarytimes.com/hero/45659.
325. "Endowment Fund Beeby Memorial; For Baby Care Department at Memorial," *Alton Evening Telegraph*, April 28, 1945, 1.
326. "A War Hero Tips His Wings to the Future," *Alton Telegraph*, April 12, 2007.
327. United States, World War II Draft Cards, 1940–1947, "Donald Reed Brooks," http://www.ancestry.com.
328. Cyrille LeBlance and Colonel Thomas F. Flynn, *Gardner in World War II* (Gardner, MA: Memorial Press, Levi Heywood Memorial Library, 1947).
329. California Birth Index, 1905–1995, "William E Burckhalter," http://www.ancestry.com.
330. Philip G. Reed, "1 Against 3, Navy Flier Sallies Forth and Jap Sallys Drop 1-2-3," *Knickerbocker News*, May 11, 1944, A-9.
331. "Lt. Bill Burckhalter 'Presumably Dead'; Details Reveal Terrific Enemy Action," *Hastings News*, 1.
332. "Charles Duell," *Brookfield Courier*, January 20, 1944, 5.
333. "Lieut. Charles Duell Died Leading His Platoon," *Brookfield Courier*, March 30, 1944, 1.
334. "Lt. Duell Awarded Army Silver Star," *Rome Daily Sentinel*, April 27, 1944, 16.
335. United States, World War II Draft Cards, 1940–1947, "Richard Ives East," http://www.ancestry.com.
336. "Colgate Honors Former Student; New Loan Fund Bears Name of Lt. East Who Died in Action Over Tunisia," *Rome Daily Sentinel*, January 20, 1945, 6.
337. "Three More Colgate Airmen Are Missing," Madison County Leader, May 13, 1943, 5.
338. "Colgate Honors Former Student," 6.
339. "Man's Best Friend; General Eisenhower Overrules Separation of Pilot and Dog," *Albany Times-Union*, June 6, 1943, A-3.

340. Ibid., A-3.
341. "Colgate Honors Former Student," 6.
342. "Hospital Head's Son Is Missing in Action," *Binghamton Press*, February 7, 1945, 5.
343. "Memorial Gift Honors Captain," *Binghamton Press*, June 21, 1945, 17.
344. "Posthumous Star for R.S. Gregory," *Binghamton Press*, April 20, 1945, 28.
345. "Charles J. Husted," *Daily News* (Tarrytown, NY), March 10, 1939, 12.
346. "Ensign Husted Listed as Dead," *Daily News* (Tarrytown, NY), February 4, 1946, 2.
347. "Husted Passes Primary Course," *Daily News* (Tarrytown, NY), January 4, 1943, 2.
348. "Ensign Husted Listed as Dead," 2.
349. Ibid.
350. United States, World War II Draft Cards, 1940–1947, "Paul Clinton MacDonald, Jr.," http://www.ancestry.com.
351. "Lt. MacDonald of Marines Killed in Battle," *Daily Argus* (Mount Vernon, NY), August 30, 1944, 2.
352. "Military Rites Here For S 1/C Clayton McClintock," *New Berlin Gazette*, October 21, 1948, 1.
353. "More Official Data Received Here on McClintock Death," *Hamilton Republican*, February 22, 1945.
354. "Dies in Service, Dennis Joseph McDonald," *Hamilton Republican*, March 29, 1945, 1.
355. "Military Funeral Planned for Dennis J. McDonald," *Utica Daily Press*, November 2, 1948, 7.
356. United States, Headstone Applications for Military Veterans, 1925–1970, "Marsh W. Miller, Jr.," http://www.ancestry.com.
357. "Binghamton Youth Receives 'Wings' for Naval Air Force; Will Go to Pearl Harbor Base; Marsh W. Miller Is Second from City to Win Flying Promotion," *Binghamton Press*, December 15, 1938, 3.
358. "Ferry Hop," *Flying and Popular Aviation* (May 1941).
359. "Ensign Marsh W. Miller, Jr., Is First Binghamton Officer Reported Missing in Action; Central Graduate in Navy Air Corps; Wife Gets Telegram," *Binghamton Press*, January 8, 1942, 10.
360. "Details of Naval Airman's Death at Start of War Are Finally Disclosed by Navy; Marsh W. Miller Believed First Officer of Area Killed," *Binghamton Press*, November 14, 1945, 3.
361. "Colgate to Give Hero Airman Campus Burial," *Binghamton Press*, May 19, 1949, 21.

362. "Lt. Phil Miller Reported Killed in Action," *Penn Yan Democrat*, August 11, 1944, 1.
363. "One of Two Survivors Tells of Fortress Loss Which Killed Lt. Miller," *Chronicle Express* (Penn Yan), July 19, 1945, 1-A.
364. Ibid.
365. "Last Spring…," *Chronicle Express* (Penn Yan), October 4, 1951, 1-B.
366. United States, World War II Draft Cards, 1940–1947, "William Starling Rising, Jr.," http://www.ancestry.com.
367. "Ridings' Baby Is in Bronxville; Funeral of Parents on Monday," Daily Argus, September 8, 1945, 12.
368. "Brooklyn Flier Wins 2 Medals for Heroic Feats," *Brooklyn Eagle*, May 27, 1945, 20.
369. "William Starling Rising' Navy Cross," Military Times, https://valor.militarytimes.com/hero/21492.
370. "Brooklyn Flier," 20.
371. "Ridings' Baby Is in Bronxville," 12.
372. "Gave Supreme Sacrifice on January 12th," *Wellsboro Gazette*, February 15, 1945, 1.
373. "Lt. T.L. Rockwell Describes Exhibition Jump," *Wellsboro Gazette*, July 13, 1944, 4.
374. "Gave Supreme Sacrifice on January 12th," 1.
375. "LT. Sinclair Killed Somewhere in Italy; Family Receives Telegram Announcing Death of Waterville Girl's Husband," *Waterville Times*, January 13, 1944, 1.
376. "Earlville," *A Book of Remembrance*, from the Wives and Mothers Club, 26.
377. U.S. Census Bureau, 1940, *Sixteenth Census of the United States: 1940—Population*, "District 27-19, Hamilton, Madison County, New York," Sheet 6B, http://www.ancestry.com.
378. United States, World War II Draft Cards, 1940–1947, "Robert Soule Swan," http://www.ancestry.com.
379. "Colgate Man Is Cited for Sinking Sub; Lt. Robert S. Swan Dropped Bombs on Boat in South Atlantic," *Syracuse Herald Journal*, March 17, 1943, 13.
380. "Former Resident Missing in Action," *Amsterdam Evening Recorder*, July 30, 1943, 10.
381. United States, World War II Draft Cards, 1940–1947, "Charles Wallace Tribken," http://www.ancestry.com.
382. "R.A.F. Citation Reveals Daring of Boro Flier; Communique Details Exploits He Never Mentions in Letters," *Brooklyn Eagle*, October 22, 1941, 7.

383. "Boro, L.I. 'Eagles' Win Glory in Malta Defense; Tribken and Mooney Blast Sicilian Field," *Brooklyn Eagle*, April 24, 1942, 20.
384. "RAF Vet Gone 4 Years Drops in on His Ma," *Brooklyn Eagle*, February 6, 1943, 3.
385. "Capt. Tribken, R.A.F and U.S. Hero, to Be Buried Tomorrow," *Brooklyn Eagle*, September 8, 1948, 19.
386. "RAF Vet Gone 4 Years Drops in on His Ma," 3.
387. "Boro Air Hero Hails 'Bomb Berlin' Drive," *Brooklyn Eagle*, February 12, 1943, 20.
388. United States, World War II Draft Cards, 1940–1947, "Robert George Waghorn," http://www.ancestry.com.
389. "PFC. R.G. Waghorn Expires in Canada," *Rome Daily Sentinel*, January 28, 1943, 6.
390. Ibid.
391. U.S. Census Bureau, 1940, *Sixteenth Census of the United States: 1940—Population*, "District 9-40, Earlville, Chenango County, New York," Sheet 2B, http://www.ancestry.com.
392. "Earlville," *Book of Remembrance*, 27.
393. United States, World War II Draft Cards, 1940–1947, "Eugene James Parteko," http://www.ancestry.com.
394. "Killed in Action," *Earlville Standard*, November 23, 1944, 1.
395. U.S. Census Bureau, 1920, *Fourteenth Census of the United States: 1920—Population*, "District 116, Canastota, Madison County, New York," Sheet 17A, http://www.ancestry.com.
396. United States, World War II Draft Cards, 1940–1947, "Frederick Floyd Riggall," http://www.ancestry.com.
397. "Lebanon," *A Book of Remembrance*, from the Wives and Mothers Club, 78.
398. "Seaman Ackerman Killed in Action; Young Man, 19, Is Second Village Resident Lost in Present War," *Rome Daily Sentinel*, December 19, 1942, 6.
399. "Ackerman Gives Life; Killed in Action at Sea," *Canastota Bee Journal*, December 25, 1942, 1.
400. "Joseph Buda Dies in War; Family Gets Telegram; Killed in Action in Italy, on Sept. 17," *Canastota Bee-Journal*, October 13, 1944, 1.
401. "Clockville Soldier Seriously Wounded," *Madison County-Times*, October 20, 1944, 5.
402. "Pvt. C.W. Cordell Dies of Wounds; Paratrooper, Lost Sept. 26, Wounded in Holland Six Days Earlier," *Rome Daily Sentinel*, October 31, 1944, 6.

403. "Pvt. Cordell Is Badly Wounded in Holland Area," *Canastota Bee-Journal*, October 20, 1944, 1.
404. United States, World War II Draft Cards, 1940–1947, "George Carlton Cox," http://www.ancestry.com.
405. "Two More Gold Stars for Canastota; Sgt. George Cox Killed in Action in Italy," *Canastota Bee-Journal*, June 9, 1944, 1.
406. "Staff Sergeant; George Cox," *Canastota Bee-Journal*, April 16, 1943, 7.
407. "Routs Out Snipers; SGT. George Cox," *Canastota Bee-Journal*, April 28, 1944, 7.
408. "Sergeant George C. Cox Canastota Dies in Italy; His Brave Deed Recalled," *Oneida Daily Dispatch*, June 5, 1944, 6.
409. "Killed In Action; Mourn Ward Davidson; Killed on Anzio Front," *Canastota Bee-Journal*, May 12, 1944, 1.
410. "In Italy; PVT. F.W. Davidson," *Canastota Bee-Journal*, January 21, 1944, 7.
411. "Killed in Action; Mourn Ward Davidson," 1.
412. "PVT Di Vincenzo Killed in Action on Italy Front," *Canastota Bee-Journal*, October 13, 1944, 1.
413. U.S. Census Bureau, 1920, *Fourteenth Census of the United States: 1920—Population*, "District 116, Canastota, Madison County, New York," Sheet 17A, http://www.ancestry.com.
414. "Lt. Farrington Is Reported as Killed in Action," *Canastota Bee-Journal*, September 22, 1944, 1.
415. "Lt. Farrington Prisoner of War," *Rome Daily Sentinel*, March 31, 1944, 6.
416. "Gold Star Veterans of Lenox in World War II," *Canastota-Bee Journal*, November 14, 1947, 3.
417. "Lt. Farrington Is Given Purple Heart by Award," *Canastota Bee-Journal*, November 10, 1944, 1.
418. "Pvt. C.R. Hayden Dies in England; 27-Year-Old Soldier Succumbs to Injuries Received in Accident," *Rome Daily Sentinel*, June 6, 1944, 6.
419. "Two More Gold Stars for Canastota; Pvt. Carroll Hayden Died in War Accident," *Canastota Bee-Journal*, June 9, 1944, 1.
420. "Gen. Ulio Writes on Pvt. Hayden's Death," *Canastota Bee-Journal*, September 1, 1944, 1.
421. United States, World War II Draft Cards, 1940–1947, "Lyle Charles Hendrickson," http://www.ancestry.com.
422. "Canastotan Is Killed on Italy Front; Parents Notified of Death Jan. 16 of PFC Lyle C. Hendrickson," *Syracuse Herald-Journal*, March 6, 1944, 10.

423. "Another War Death Here; Lyle Hendrickson Is Victim; Family Gets Word He Is Killed in Action in Italy," *Canastota Bee-Journal*, March 3, 1944, 1.
424. "With Invasion Army; Pvt. Lyle Hendrickson," *Canastota Bee-Journal*, December 3, 1943, 7.
425. "PFC Hendrickson Killed by Shell in His Fox-Hole," *Canastota Bee-Journal*, June 2, 1944, 1.
426. "Chaplain Pays Tribute to PFC. L. Hendrickson," *Canastota Bee-Journal*, February 23, 1945, 1.
427. "PFC. Lyle Hendrickson Is Given Purple Heart Award Posthumously," *Canastota Bee-Journal*, April 14, 1944, 1.
428. "Cyril Hendrickson," *Madison County Times*, October 22, 1943, 3.
429. United States, World War II Draft Cards, 1940–1947, "Vincent Anthony Lomonaco," http://www.ancestry.com.
430. "V. Lomanaco Dies in War; Killed on Italian Front; Family Receives Word of His Death Oct. 30," *Canastota Bee-Journal*, November 17, 1944, 1.
431. "See Sights in Italy; PVC. Vincent A. Lomanaco," *Canastota Bee-Journal*, October 20, 1944, 7.
432. "Plane Crash Kills Maula; Army Flier Died Friday," *Canastota Bee-Journal*, December 22, 1944, 1.
433. "Anthony Maula," *Canastota Bee-Journal*, October 22, 1943, 7.
434. United States, Headstone Application for Military Veterans, 1925–1963, "Anthony Maula," http://www.ancestry.com.
435. "Middleditch's Body Arrives for Burial; Funeral Services for 1st of County War Dead Arranged," *Rome Daily Sentinel*, October 28, 1947, 8.
436. "Marine Killed in the Pacific; Private, First Class, Gardner Middleditch Lived at Canastota," *Oneida Daily Dispatch*, December 7, 1944, 5.
437. "Pfc. Middleditch Is Reported Dead in Pacific Area," *Canastota Bee-Journal*, December 8, 1944, 1.
438. "Lt. Narehood Declared Dead by War Dept," *Rome Sentinel*, August 11, 1945, 2.
439. U.S. Census Bureau, 1940, *Sixteenth Census of the United States: 1940—Population*, "District 27-30, Lenox, Madison County, New York," Sheet 6B, http://www.ancestry.com.
440. "Lt. C.B. Narehood Missing in France; Verona High School Alumnus Has Been Overseas Since October '43," *Rome Daily Sentinel*, August 29, 1944, 2.

441. "Lt. C.B. Narehood Gets Silver Star, Gallantry Cited, Lt. C.B. Narehood; Forced to Crash Land in Enemy Territory," *Rome Daily Sentinel*, January 20, 1945, 2.
442. "Frank Penna," *Oneida Dispatch*, September 9, 2016, http://www.oneidadispatch.com.
443. "Private Penna Killed in Action," *Rome Daily Sentinel*, December 27, 1943, 6.
444. "Frank Penna Died a Hero; Letter from Army Associate Tells How He Lost Life," *Canastota Bee-Journal*, February 4, 1944, 1.
445. Elizabeth Doran, "CNY Family Had 'Given Up Hope' for Return of WWII Marine Who Comes Home Thursday," September 13, 2016, http://www.syracuse.com/news/index.ssf/2016/09/cny_family_had_given_up_hope_for_return_of_missing_wwii_marine.html.
446. "Two Madison Co. Fliers Reported Missing in Flights Over Europe," *Madison County Times*, April 19, 1945, 5.
447. "Sgt. Roberts Is Missing; Was Wampsville Youth; Was Lost on Bombing Mission Over France," *Canastota Bee-Journal*, April 14, 1944, 1.
448. "Gold Star Veterans of Lenox in World War II," *Canastota-Bee Journal*, November 14, 1947, 3.
449. "Bob Sayers War Victim; Was in US Navy 11 Years; First Canastota Boy to Make Supreme Sacrifice," *Canastota Bee-Journal*, November 6, 1942, 1.
450. "Lt. Tells of Bob Sayers; With Him on Last Flight; Mrs. Peach Gives Us Report on Son's Death," *Canastota Bee-Journal*, June 4, 1943, 1.
451. U.S. Census Bureau, 1940, *Sixteenth Census of the United States: 1940—Population*, "District 27-26, Lenox, Madison County, New York," Sheet 8B, http://www.ancestry.com.
452. "PFC Tornatore Listed Missing Since Dec. 20th," *Canastota Bee-Journal*, January 19, 1945, 1.
453. United States, Headstone and Interment Records for U.S. Military Cemeteries on Foreign Soil, 1942–1949, "Carmen T Tornatore," http://www.ancestry.com.
454. "Gold Star Veterans of Lenox in World War II," *Canastota-Bee Journal*, November 14, 1947, 3.
455. United States, World War II Draft Cards, 1940–1947, "Vincent William Walters," http://www.ancestry.com.
456. "T/Cpl. Vincent Walters Is Reported Wounded," *Rome Daily Sentinel*, June 27, 1944, 6.

457. U.S. Census Bureau, 1940, *Sixteenth Census of the United States: 1940—Population*, "District 27-29, Lenox, Madison County, New York," Sheet 2A, http://www.ancestry.com.
458. "Soldier Dies in Normandy," *Utica Daily Press*, July 12, 1944, 7.
459. "Pfc. Nelson Drake Killed in Germany December 19," *Madison County Times*, January 12, 1945, 5.
460. U.S. Census Bureau, 1940, *Sixteenth Census of the United States: 1940—Population*, "District 27-1944, Lenox, Madison County, New York," Sheet 8A, http://www.ancestry.com.
461. United States, Social Security Applications and Claims Index, 1936–2007, "Dorothy Mary Ano," http://www.ancestry.com.
462. "The Legion to Honor Returning War Heroes," *Mid-York Weekly*, October 30, 1947, 1.
463. "Clockville Soldier Killed in Action," *Madison County Times*, August 11, 1944, 3.
464. "Memorial Service Held for Ph.M. Donald Phipps," *Rome Daily Sentinel*, December 21, 1944, 13.
465. "Don Phipps Died in War; Killed in Guam Action," *Canastota Bee-Journal*, August 18, 1944, 1.
466. "Clockville Hero's Body Arrives in USA," *Madison County Times*, March 26, 1948, 1.
467. "Letter Gives Details," *Canastota Bee-Journal*, September 22, 1944, 7.
468. "Donald Phipps," *Rome Daily Sentinel*, February 21, 1944, 13.
469. New York, US Index to Death Certificates, 1862–1948, "Eugene Francis Clair," http://www.ancestry.com.
470. U.S. Census Bureau, 1940, *Sixteenth Census of the United States: 1940—Population*, "District 27-34, Madison, Madison County, New York," Sheet 3A, http://www.ancestry.com.
471. "Madison," *A Book of Remembrance*, from the Wives and Mothers Club, 93.
472. "Solsville Veteran Dies in Hospital," *Waterville Times*, June 15, 1944, 3.
473. United States, World War II Draft Cards, 1940–1947, "John Beverly McMullin," http://www.ancestry.com.
474. "S/Sgt. McMullen Being Brought Home for Burial," *Cortland Standard*, October 21, 1948, 2.
475. "Madison," *Book of Remembrance*, 94.
476. U.S., Headstone Applications for Military Veterans, 1925–1970, "Charles F. Blanke, Jr.," http://www.ancestry.com.
477. "Flyer Killed; 2 St. Louisans Killed in Bomber Crashes," *St. Louis Post Dispatch*, January 17, 1945, 12A.

478. "B-17 Crashes in Nelson—Parachutist Is Killed," *Cazenovia Republican*, January 18, 1945, 1.
479. New York Birth Index, 1881–1942, "Robert E. Schantz," http://www.ancestry.com.
480. "Pvt. Schantz for Second Time Reported Killed," *Cazenovia Republican*, February 4, 1943, 4.
481. U.S. Census Bureau, 1940, *Sixteenth Census of the United States: 1940—Population*, "District 27-36, Nelson, Madison County, New York," Sheet 1B, http://www.ancestry.com.
482. "Pvt. Schantz for Second Time," 4.
483. "Robert Schantz Awarded Purple Heart Posthumously," *Cazenovia Republican*, December 2, 1943, 4.
484. United States, World War II Draft Cards, 1940–1947, "Raymond Vernon Allen," http://www.ancestry.com.
485. "Technical Sergeant Raymond V. Allen Missing in Action," *Community Commando* (January–February 1945): 5.
486. "T-SGT. R.V. Allen Reported Killed; Liberator Pilot Was Listed Missing Nov. 9, 1944, on 28th Mission," *Rome Daily Sentinel*, May 14, 1945, 6.
487. "Raymond V. Allen Now Reported as Dead," *Madison County Times*, May 18, 1945, 5.
488. United States, World War II Draft Cards, 1940–1947, "Joseph Arthur Baldanza," http://www.ancestry.com.
489. "Lt. Baldanza Dies in Crash in N. Africa; Former Syracusan Has Five Brothers Serving in Navy," *Syracuse Herald-Journal*, January 29, 1944, 3.
490. "Bodies of Four Local Boys Coming Home," *Madison County Times*, May 21, 1948, 1.
491. United States, World War II Draft Cards, 1940–1947, "Paul Gocht Ballard," http://www.ancestry.com.
492. "Lt. P.G. Ballard Declared Dead," *Rome Sentinel*, February 25, 1946, 6.
493. New York Birth Index, 1881–1942, "George J Bellinger," http://www.ancestry.com.
494. "Lieutenant Bellinger Is Reported Missing; Formerly of O. Castle," *Oneida Daily Dispatch*, June 13, 1942, 1.
495. "Bellinger-Robinson," *Albany Evening News*, August 4, 1932, 13.
496. U.S. Census Bureau, 1940, *Sixteenth Census of the United States: 1940—Population*, "District 17-20, Pensacola, Escambia County, Florida," Sheet 2A, http://www.ancestry.com.
497. "World War II Veteran Dies at Batavia; Served in England and France in Gen. Patton's Army," *Rome Sentinel*, September 25, 1945, 6.

498. "Bruno Taken Ill in France Is Dead; Oneida Man, 22, Dies in Hospital at Batavia," *Syracuse Herald-Journal*, September 25, 1945, 4.
499. "DFC Awarded R.D. Buscher," *Rome Sentinel*, June 18, 1946, 6.
500. "Oneida Sailor Reported Missing," *Utica Daily Press*, August 7, 1945, 5.
501. "DFC Warded R.D Buscher," 6.
502. United States, World War II Draft Cards, 1940–1947, "William James Carinci," http://www.ancestry.com.
503. "PFC William J. Carinici, Oneida, Killed in Action Fighting on French Soil," *Oneida Daily Dispatch*, September 9, 1944, 3.
504. U.S. Census Bureau, 1940, *Sixteenth Census of the United States: 1940—Population*, "District 27-45, Oneida, Madison County, New York," Sheet 5B, http://www.ancestry.com.
505. New York, New York Guard Service Cards, 1906–1918, 1940–1948, "William J. Carinci," http://www.ancestry.com.
506. "PFC William J. Carinici, Oneida," 3.
507. "William Carinci Killed in Action; Local Athlete Gives Life for Country in France Aug. 12," *Rome Daily Sentinel*, September 9, 1944, 6.
508. "Silver Star Awarded Posthumously to William J. Carinici," *Madison County Times*, June 29, 1945, 5.
509. "Transport Pilot, Lost Year Ago, Declared Dead; First Lt. Donald J. Cunningham, 22, Disappeared Near Iceland Dec. 9, 1943, While on Ferry Service," *Rome Daily Sentinel*, December 21, 1944, 7.
510. "Lt. Cunningham Now Officially Listed as Dead; War Department Informs Parents and Wife of Oneida Officer," *Oneida Daily Dispatch*, December 21, 1944, 1.
511. "Orion E. Dunster," *Madison County Times*, February 4, 1949, 5.
512. "Staff Sergeant Orion E. Dunster," *Community Commando* (December 1945): 5.
513. United States, World War II Draft Cards, 1940–1947, "Alexander Bruce Durkee," http://www.ancestry.com.
514. "Mustang Pilot Wins Air Medal; Lt. A.B. Durkee Completes 25 Missions; Unit Won President's Citation," *Rome Daily Sentinel*, November 15, 1944, 6.
515. "Lt. A.B. Durkee Is Awarded Silver Star; Fighter Pilot Has Been Missing Since Jan. 15," *Rome Daily Sentinel*, August 6, 1945, 6.
516. "Military Rites for Lt. Durkee Set for Monday," *Rome Sentinel*, April 15, 1949, 9.
517. "Oneida Marine Killed Abroad; Private First Class Donald Dwight Earl Met Death on Okinawa," *Oneida Daily Dispatch*, May 23, 1945, 2.

518. "7 War Dead on Way Home for Burial," *Utica Daily Press*, January 19, 1949, 3.
519. "Capt. Wilbur Earl of Kenwood Killed in Action, France," *Madison County Times*, October 27, 1944, 5.
520. "Capt. W.N. Earl Killed in France; Former Oneida Ltd. Salesman Over Three Years; Kenwood Native," *Rome Daily Sentinel*, October 20, 1944, 6.
521. "Captain Wilber N. Earl," *Community Commando* (December 1945): 5.
522. "LT. F.R. Gowing Declared Dead; Mustang Pilot Reported Missing Aug. 2, 1944; Former Rome Worker," *Rome Daily Sentinel*, January 9, 1945, 6.
523. "Sgt. D.C. Harrington Reported Killed in Action in Africa," *Rome Daily Sentinel*, April 12, 1943, 6.
524. "Strikes Disgust Soldier at Front; Sgt. Harrington, Killed in Tunisia, Wrote Thus in Last Letter," *Rome Daily Sentinel*, May 1, 1943, 6.
525. "Harrington Awarded Star," *Rome Daily Sentinel*, August 18, 1945, 9.
526. "Donald C. Harrington, Silver Star," *Military Times*, https://valor.militarytimes.com/hero/56790.
527. "Bodies of Four Local Boys Coming Home," *Madison County Times*, May 21, 1948, 1.
528. United States, World War II Draft Cards, 1940–1947, "Raymond Francis Harsma," http://www.ancestry.com.
529. "Albany Wife Told Ensign Is Missing," Albany Times Union, July 14, 1944, 12.
530. "Albany Ensign Missing at Sea," *Knickerbocker News*, July 14, 1944, 1.
531. New York Marriage Index, 1881–1967, "Raymond F Harsma," http://www.ancestry.com.
532. "Private Hasty Ends His Life Near North Bay; Body of Oneida Soldier Discovered by Stepfather on His Farm," *Oneida Daily Dispatch*, September 22, 1944, 2.
533. United States, World War II Draft Cards, 1940–1947, "Robert Leo Hollis," http://www.ancestry.com.
534. "Lt. Robt. Hollis, Missing Over a Year, Found Beside Wrecked Plane Near Twin Lakes," *Madison County Times*, November 1, 1946, 6.
535. "Robert L. Hollis; Aviation Cadet, US Navy," *Oneida Dispatch*, April 19, 1944, 2.
536. "Robert L. Hollis Wins Commission," *Rome Daily Sentinel*, March 20, 1945, 6.
537. "Lt. R.L. Hollis Will Take Bride at Port Washington," *Rome Daily Sentinel*, March 21, 1945, 6.

538. "Pilot's Body Found Near Twin Lakes; Lt. Robert Hollis Lost in Flight to RAAF in 1945," *Rome Daily Sentinel*, October 29, 1946, 2.
539. New York, World War II Enlisted Men Cards, 1940–1945, "Robert M. Howd," http://www.ancestry.com.
540. "Robert M. Howd Dies in Europe; Former Oneida Newspaper Carrier Missing Since July 12 Over Yugoslavia," *Oneida Daily Dispatch*, September 2, 1944, 1.
541. "Pfc. Stewart A. Jones, 21, Reported Missing in Action," *Rome Daily Sentinel*, June 2, 1942, 6.
542. *Rome Daily Sentinel*, August 15, 1945, 5.
543. U.S. Census Bureau, 1940, *Sixteenth Census of the United States: 1940—Population*, "District 21-43, Sausalito, Marin County, California," Sheet 25B, http://www.ancestry.com.
544. "Corporal Jones Declared Dead After 2 Years; But Parents of Oneida Soldier at Corregidor Keep Up Hope," *Oneida Daily Dispatch*, May 17, 1944, 1.
545. "Identity of Cpl. Jones Established; Quartermaster General Informs Next of Kin," *Rome Daily Sentinel*, June 11, 1947, 8.
546. United States, World War II Draft Cards, 1940–1947, "James Vincent Latteri," http://www.ancestry.com.
547. "Seaman Latteri Is Victim of Crash; Former Garageman Killed Near Rochester; Was Stationed at Sampson," *Rome Daily Sentinel*, July 1, 1943, 6.
548. New York Marriage Index, 1881–1967, "James V. Latteri," http://www.ancestry.com.
549. New York Birth Index, 1881–1942, "James V. Latteri," http://www.ancestry.com.
550. *Rome Daily Sentinel*, July 1, 1943, 6.
551. "Oneida Man, Sailor, Dies in Collision," *Utica Observer-Dispatch*, July 1, 1943, 6-A.
552. United States, World War II Draft Cards, 1940–1947, "Donald Leon MacArthur," http://www.ancestry.com.
553. "Captain Lost on a Mission; Donald MacArthur, with Relatives in Oneida, Reported Missing," *Oneida Dispatch*, February 29, 1944, 3.
554. "Lt. MacArthur Tells of Raids on Jap Islands Grandson of John MacArthur Awarded Air Medal for Heroism," *Oneida Daily Dispatch*, August 27, 1943, 8.
555. *Oneida Dispatch*, February 29, 1944, 3.

556. "Richard Charles Perling, 20, Reported Killed in Action; Popular Three-Letter High School Athlete Was Radioman in U.S. Navy," *Oneida Daily Dispatch*, September 14, 1942, 1.
557. "Memorial Is Held for R.C. Perling; Over 200 Attend Service for Radioman Lost in Action in Solomons Area," *Rome Daily Sentinel*, December 7, 1942, 6.
558. "Sgt. Pflanz Killed in Germany," *Utica Daily Press*, March 19, 1945, 10.
559. U.S. Census Bureau, 1940, *Sixteenth Census of the United States: 1940—Population*, "District 27-45, Oneida, Madison County, New York," Sheet 3A, http://www.ancestry.com.
560. New York Marriage Index, 1881–1967, "Arthur C. Pflanz," http://www.ancestry.com.
561. United States, World War II Army Enlistment Records, 1938–1946, "Arthur C Pflanz," http://www.ancestry.com.
562. "Sgt. A.C. Pflanz Killed in Action; Young Man, Previously Reported Missing, Lost in Battle Dec. 3," *Rome Daily Sentinel*, March 16, 1945, 6.
563. United States, World War II Draft Cards, 1940–1947, "Arlington Coulter Raymond," http://www.ancestry.com.
564. "Arlington Raymond Missing in Action," *Rome Daily Sentinel*, April 24, 1945, 6.
565. New York Marriage Index, 1881–1967, "Arlington C. Raymond," http://www.ancestry.com.
566. "Arlington Raymond Missing in Action," *Rome Daily Sentinel*, April 24, 1945, 6.
567. U.S. Census Bureau, 1940, *Sixteenth Census of the United States: 1940—Population*, "District 27-41, Oneida, Madison County, New York," Sheet 12A, http://www.ancestry.com.
568. "State Bridge Soldier Killed in Germany," *Madison County Times*, May 18, 1945, 5.
569. "Arlington C. Raymond, Silver Star Citation," Military Times, https://valor.militarytimes.com/hero/115230.
570. New York Birth Index, 1881–1942, "Jonah Reeves," http://www.ancestry.com.
571. "Flight Officer J.B. Reeves Declared Officially Dead; Oneidan Missing in Overseas Operation from England Since July 4, 1943," *Oneida Daily Dispatch*, May 19, 1944, 1.
572. Canada, World War II Service Files of War Dead, 1939–1947, "Jonah Bruce Reeves," http://www.ancestry.com.

573. "Jonah Reeves, Hamilton Student, Enlists in Canada," *Rome Daily Sentinel*, October 24, 1941, 6.
574. "Flight Officer J.B. Reeves," 1.
575. "SGT. Roney Dies of Gunshot Would; Young Man Killed in Accident at Texas Camp; Was Coach Line Driver," *Rome Daily Sentinel*, October 18, 1943, 6.
576. Texas Death Certificates, 1903–1982, "Robert C. Roney," http://www.ancestry.com.
577. "Pfc. J.C. Rule, 27, Killed in Action; Had Won Purple Heart and Combat Badge; Was Wounded Augt. 12," *Rome Daily Sentinel*, January 8, 1945, 6.
578. *Rome Daily Sentinel*, October 7, 1941, 6.
579. "Rule-Panzica," *Madison County Times*, January 12, 1945.
580. United States, World War II Draft Cards, 1940–1947, "Joseph Thomas Sansone," http://www.ancestry.com.
581. "Sgt. Thomas Sansone Killed Aboard Boat Enroute Home," *Madison County Times*, August 31, 1945, 5.
582. "Last Rites Held for CPL Sansone; Army Chaplain Pays Tribute to Soldier Who Died Aboard Transport," *Oswego Palladium Times*, August 30, 1945, 5.
583. United States, World War II Draft Cards, 1940–1947, "Robert Hewitt Seifert," http://www.ancestry.com.
584. "Lt. R.H. Seifert Declared Dead," *Rome Daily Sentinel*, November 21, 1945, 6.
585. "Williamstown and Oneida Soldiers Get Pilot Wings," *Rome Daily Sentinel*, October 11, 1943, 7.
586. *Rome Daily Sentinel*, November 21, 1945, 6.
587. "Memorial Is Held for LT. N.R. Short," *Rome Daily Sentinel*, August 21, 1943, 5.
588. "Plant Holds Memorial Rites for 3," *Utica Daily Press*, October 13, 1943, 11a.
589. "Memorial Is Held for LT. N.R. Short," 5.
590. "Mother Receives Medal Awarded Posthumously," *Brookfield Courier*, October 27, 1943, 1.
591. New York World War II Enlisted Men Cards, 1940–1945, "Thomas W. Skinner, Jr.," http://www.ancestry.com.
592. "Sgt. T.W. Skinner Killed in Action: Former Co. K Member Loses Life in Italy; Wife in Dallas, Texas," *Rome Daily Sentinel*, March 27, 1945, 6.

593. U.S. Census Bureau, 1940, *Sixteenth Census of the United States: 1940—Population*, "District 33-92, Vernon, Oneida County, New York," Sheet 8B, http://www.ancestry.com.
594. "Sgt. T.W. Skinner Killed in Action," 6.
595. New York Birth Index, 1881–1942, "James G Townsend," http://www.ancestry.com.
596. "Letter Received from Paratrooper Killed in Action June 7, 1944," *Community Commando* (January–February 1945): 5.
597. "Pvt. Van Auken Dies of Wounds; Injured in Action with 7th Army in Germany; Was Hurt in Training," *Rome Daily Sentinel*, March 6, 1945, 6.
598. United States, Headstone Application for Military Veterans, 1925–1963, "Richard N. Van Nostrand," http://www.ancestry.com.
599. "Staff Sergeant Richard N. Van Nostrand Killed in Action in Philippines," *Community Commando* (January–February 1945): 5.
600. "Staff Sergeant Richard Van Nostrand Commended for Courageous Action," *Community Commando* (August 28, 1943): 3.
601. "Oneidan Killed in Philippines; Staff Sergt. Richard N. Van Nostrand Lost Life in Enemy Action," *Oneida Daily Dispatch*, December 26, 1944, 3.
602. "Louis H. Veling, 2nd Lieutenant, Reported Killed; Oneidan in Transport Service Between India and China," *Oneida Daily Dispatch*, March 30, 1944, 1.
603. "Lt. Louis H. Veling," *Community Commando* (August 28, 1943).
604. "Awards Made Posthumously; Lt. Louis Veling's Widow Given Air Medal and Oak Leaf Cluster," *Oneida Daily Dispatch*, August 28, 1944, 2.
605. United States, World War II Draft Cards, 1940–1947, "Charles Blanchard Watkins," http://www.ancestry.com.
606. "To Hold Services for Lt. Watkins," *Rome Daily Sentinel*, September 20, 1945, 6.
607. U.S. Census Bureau, 1940, *Sixteenth Census of the United States: 1940—Population*, "District 27-46, Oneida, Madison County, New York," Sheet 6B, http://www.ancestry.com.
608. "Infant Dies," *Utica Daily Press*, November 29, 1944, 12.
609. "Watkins Completes Course," *Oneida Daily Dispatch*, July 26, 1943, 5.
610. "Laverne Austin of Fenner Killed in Action," *Madison County Times*, December 26, 1941, 1.
611. New York Birth Index, 1881–1942, "Robert Stratton," http://www.ancestry.com.
612. "Eaton," *Book of Remembrance*, 41.

613. United States, World War II Draft Cards, 1940–1947, "Harry Thomas Cronin," http://www.ancestry.com.
614. "T/SGT. Harry Cronin Killed in Action in Germany," *Community Commando* (May 1945): 5.
615. "The Legion to Honor Returning War Heroes," *Mid-York Weekly*, November 20, 1947, 4.
616. United States, World War II Draft Cards, 1940–1947, "Lester Woodrow Thurston," http://www.ancestry.com.
617. "Family Makes Arrangements for War Dead," *Rome Daily Sentinel*, March 31, 1948, 8.
618. United States, World War II Draft Cards, 1940–1947, "James Lyndon Case," http://www.ancestry.com.
619. "Cpl. James L. Case Killed in Action on Iwo Jima," *Madison County Times*, March 30, 1945, 1.
620. Ibid., 1.
621. "Private James Lynn Case," *Madison County Times*, February 12, 1943, 1.
622. "Cpl. James L. Case," 1.
623. "PFC Desormeau Killed in Action," *Rome Daily Sentinel*, November 8, 1943, 6.
624. "Chittenango Soldier Dies in Italy War: PFC. Desormeau Served with Chemical Unit, Brother Here Says," *Syracuse Herald-Journal*, November 8, 1943, 4.
625. New York Birth Index, 1881–1942, "Warren E. Hayward," http://www.ancestry.com.
626. "Navy Reported Perryville Boy Lost in Action," *Canastota Bee-Journal*, July 30, 1943, 1.
627. "Senior Officer Says No Trace Found of Warren Hayward," *Cazenovia Republican*, January 13, 1944, 4.
628. "PFC. John H. Kay," *Madison County Times*, November 16, 1945, 1.
629. "Crash of B-29 Spraying DDT Killed John Kay," *Clinton Courier*, November 29, 1945, 1.
630. United States, World War II Draft Cards, 1940–1947, "Harry Carl Kinnetz," http://www.ancestry.com.
631. "Chittenango Station," *Madison County Times*, August 30, 1929, 3.
632. "Harry C. Kinnetz," *Madison County Times*, August 14, 1942, 5.
633. "S/SGT. Harry Kinnetz, Chittenango, Missing," *Rome Daily Sentinel*, March 4, 1944, 6.
634. "Chittenango Station," *Madison County Times*, July 7, 1948, 1.

635. United States, World War II Draft Cards, 1940–1947, "Harold Eugene Sage," http://www.ancestry.com.
636. "Corp. Harold Sage," *Gazette & Farmers' Journal*, June 23, 1949, 6.
637. "Soldier's Widow Gave Birth to Daughter," *Madison County Times*, September 3, 1943, 1.
638. "Funeral Rites for CPL. Sage Saturday," *Gazette & Farmers' Journal* (Baldwinsville, NY), June 23, 1949, 1.
639. United States, World War II Draft Cards, 1940–1947, "Peter Cornelius Sleight," http://www.ancestry.com.
640. "Funeral Saturday for PFC. Peter C. Sleight," *Madison County Times*, April 29, 1949, 1.
641. "Kenneth Winnie Brought Home," *Madison County Times*, October 20, 1948, 1.
642. "Kenneth Winnie Killed on Luzon," *Madison County Times*, June 22, 1945, 1.
643. "Kenneth Winnie Tells of Trip to Hawaii," *Madison County Times*, July 4, 1941, 4.
644. "Kenneth Winnie Killed on Luzon," 1.

Appendix

645. United States, World War I Draft Registration Cards, 1917–1918, "Registration Card No. 12, Gerald William Hopkins," http://www.ancestry.com.
646. New York, U.S. Death Index, 1852–1956, "Gerald W. Hopkins, " http://www.ancestry.com.
647. U.S. Census Bureau, 1910, *Thirteenth Census of the United States: 1910—Population*, "District 22, Madison, Madison County, New York," Sheet 7A, http://www.ancestry.com.
648. New York, *Abstracts of World War I Military Service*, 1917–1919, "Gerald W. Hopkins," http://www.ancestry.com.
649. United States, World War I Draft Registration Cards, 1917–1918, "Gerald W. Hopkins," http://www.ancestry.com.
650. "Last Thursday Afternoon an Official Telegram Was Received," *Waterville Times*, September 20, 1918, 1.
651. "Gerald Hopkins of Bouckville," *Madison County Times*, August 8, 1919, 2.

652. U.S. Census Bureau, 1940, *Sixteenth Census of the United States: 1940—Population*, "District 33-30, Sherrill, Oneida County, New York," Sheet 10B, http://www.ancestry.com.
653. U.S. Presbyterian Church Records, 1701–1970, "Robert Jay Lasher," http://www.ancestry.com.
654. "Robert J. Lasher," *Post-Standard*, May 4, 2018, http://www.syracuse.com.
655. "Chittenango Boy First Death in County in Jap War," *Madison County Times*, December 19, 1941, 1.
656. "Chittenango Sailor Reported Dead Is Alive," *Madison County Times*, December 26, 1941, 1.

ABOUT THE AUTHOR

Matthew Urtz was appointed Madison County Historian in April 2010. In 2013, Urtz initiated a veterans interview program that, to date, has recorded the personal experiences of more than two dozen soldiers, including fifteen World War II veterans. The program is ongoing, and the interviews are digitized on the historian's website. He lives in Oneida, New York, with his wife, Christa, and two dogs, Dolly and Martha.